Fear & Folklore: American Witches

Allen Sircy

Table of Contents

Introduction 3

History 5

The Salem Witch Trials 17

Other Witch Trials 52

Legends 86

Curses & Spells 122

Hex Breakers 143

New York Necromancers 173

Introduction

Having written nearly two dozen books delving into the haunted histories of various American cities, I've woven true tales of monsters, spiritualism, galvanism (think Frankenstein's monster), and witches into my stories. Witches, occupy a gray area in paranormal circles, captivating some while leaving others indifferent. In my opinion, the intriguing allure of witches lies in the fact that they often defy societal norms, predominantly women (and occasionally men) who are misunderstood.

While a few exploit the title for monetary gain, the majority do not embody the malevolent figures depicted in popular culture that cast evil spells or fly around on brooms.

In the early centuries of the United States, merely expressing an interest in herbs and holistic medicine could brand one as a witch. Women who chose to live alone away from other people in their village were wrongly accused and ridiculed. However, as exemplified by the tragic events in Salem, Massachusetts, simple God-fearing Puritans faced accusations that ultimately led to their death. Today, in modern times, there are still people who identify as a witch who live ordinary lives. Thankfully, they do not live in fear of being hanged for simply being different.

With the book I hope to shine a light on the mysterious and often misunderstood world of witches in the United States.

Here it is Fear & Folklore: American Witches. I hope you enjoy reading it as much as I did writing it.

History

Witches, with a history deeply rooted in ancient tales and biblical narratives, have captivated the human imagination for centuries. The first known account of a witch is the story of the Witch of Endor, a figure mentioned in the Book of Samuel in the Old Testament.

In this ancient tale, King Saul, distressed and desperate for guidance, finds himself facing the formidable Philistine army. Stricken with fear, he seeks insight from a source he had previously condemned – a so-called witch residing in the town of Endor.

According to the Book of Samuel in the Old Testament, the Witch of Endor possessed a peculiar power: the ability to summon the dead. Intrigued by the prospect of divine assistance, King Saul disguises himself and seeks out this mysterious woman. Despite his prior edicts against necromancy and magic, he implores her to bring forth the spirit of the recently departed prophet Samuel.

In a scene filled with tension and mystique, the witch follows her ancient rituals, invoking supernatural forces. To everyone's astonishment, the spirit of Samuel does appear, although the text emphasizes that the woman herself is terrified by the unexpected manifestation. Samuel's spirit delivers a haunting message to Saul, predicting his impending doom and the defeat of Israel at the hands of the Philistines.

Other Biblical verses, including Exodus 22:18 and Leviticus 19:26 condemn witches. However, Leviticus 20:27 upped the ante, seemingly calling for witches to be executed.

A man also or woman that hath a familiar spirit, or that is a wizard, shall surely be put to death: they shall stone them with stones: their blood shall be upon them.

These grim writings in the Bible helped shape early perceptions and would later come into play during the infamous witch trials that would plague Europe and the British colonies.

In the classical era, winged harpies and owl-like "strix" were added to the mystique. Circe and Medea from Greek mythology embodied witch-like enchantresses, laying the groundwork for tropes associated with witches in later centuries.

In Eastern Europe Baba Yaga, a quintessential character in Slavic folklore, is one of the most enigmatic and complex witches in global mythology. Her story, rich with symbolism and cultural significance, has been passed down through generations.

Baba Yaga's origins trace back to ancient Slavic traditions, where she is often depicted as an old, haggard woman with a fearsome appearance. She is described as having iron teeth, a long, crooked nose, and a bony, emaciated figure. Her eyes are said to be piercing, capable of seeing into the souls of those who dare to cross her path.

Baba Yaga is a complex character, embodying both malevolent and benevolent qualities. She is known for her unpredictable nature, sometimes helping lost souls who find their way to her hut, and other times devouring those who anger her. This duality makes her a symbol of the wild and untamed aspects of nature, as well as the cycles of life and death.

She possesses immense magical powers, including the ability to control the elements, fly through the air and cast spells. Her magic is deeply tied to the natural world, and she is often seen as a guardian of the forest, its creatures, and its hidden secrets.

Many tales of Baba Yaga involve young orphans who stumble upon her hut in the forest. One of the most famous stories is that of Vasilisa the Beautiful. In this tale, Vasilisa, a young girl with a cruel stepmother and stepsisters, is sent into the forest to seek Baba Yaga's aid. With the help of a magical doll given to her by her late mother, Vasilisa completes the difficult tasks set by Baba Yaga and earns the witch's grudging respect. In the end, she gains a magical skull that helps her defeat her stepmother and stepsisters, allowing her to live happily ever after.

The mid-1400s marked the rise of witch hysteria in Europe, fueled by confessions obtained under torture. Witch hunts became commonplace, with accused individuals, often marginalized women, facing execution by burning or hanging. Between 1500 and 1660, it's believed that up to 80,000 suspected witches met their demise, with Germany having the highest execution rate and Ireland the lowest.

The publication of the "Malleus Maleficarum" in 1486, a guide on identifying and hunting witches, intensified the hysteria. Labeling witchcraft as heresy, the book became a definitive authority for both Protestants and Catholics. Its popularity surpassed all books in Europe except the Bible, contributing to over a century of widespread fear and persecution.

As witchcraft gained popularity, witch hunts intensified, marking a dark chapter in history with echoes of the ancient and biblical tales that shaped the perception of witches through the ages.

In 1428, a dark cloud settled over Valais, Switzerland, as the sinister practice of witch-hunting began. Starting in Lower Valais, under the rule of the House of Savoy, the persecution extended its grasp to Upper Valais and nearby valleys, casting a shadow for eight agonizing years and claiming the lives of 367 people.

The roots of this haunting chapter were complex,

influenced by political divisions and the aftermath of the Waldensian persecution in Friborg. Triggered by rebellion and weakened Savoy rule, the witch trials first surfaced in Val Danivier and Val Daelen, south of Siders and Zion.

By the summer of 1428, the entire region felt the impact of witch-hunting. On August 7, Loik authorities formalized trial procedures, allowing even nobility to face arrest based on public gossip or accusations by three or four neighbors. Torture, reserved for victims with a certain number of accusers, became a gruesome tool for extracting confessions.

Johannes Front of Lucerne, in 1430, provided a chilling account commissioned by Christoph von Silenen. The accused faced charges ranging from murder to heresy and witchcraft, allegedly paying homage to demons as black animals. As the trials unfolded, victims confessed to flying on ointment-smeared chairs and attending Sabbaths with devilish figures preaching anti-Christian sermons.

The trials involved hundreds, with over 200 burned at the stake by 1430. Remarkably, two-thirds of the victims were male peasants. Condemnation required at least three neighbors to accuse publicly, leading to confessions of meetings with the Devil, flying, and transforming into werewolves.

Brutal executions awaited the condemned, predominantly by burning. Bags of gunpowder tied around their necks hastened their merciless demise. After subsiding in Valais and Savoy, the phenomenon spread, influencing regions like Friborg, Neuchâtel, Vevey, and Domartin, contributing to the broader wave of early modern witch trials in 16th and 17th century Western Europe. The Council of Basel from 1431 to 1437 played a role in documenting and discussing this emerging phenomenon of witchcraft.

In the 16th and 17th centuries, a pervasive fear of witchcraft gripped England and Europe, leading to trials and executions, particularly in Oxford. Although witchcraft wasn't a capital offense in Britain until 1563, suspicions were rampant. Pope Innocent VIII declared it heresy in 1484, paving the way for the torture, burning, and hanging of around 200,000 witches in Western Europe until 1750.

Most victims were elderly, poor women, often accused due to their appearance, with features like snaggle teeth and sunken cheeks seen as signs of the 'Evil Eye.' Owning a cat was considered proof of witchcraft, as these animals were thought to be witch's companions.

Henry VIII

The first English law related to witchcraft emerged during Henry VIII's reign, with earlier trials, such as the notorious case of Eleanor Cobham in 1441. James I, also James VI of Scotland, intensified trials, influenced by the Copenhagen witch trials of 1589.

In 1612, England under the rule of King James I was consumed by religious persecution and superstition. Lancashire, in particular, became a hub of sinister occurrences. King James VI of Scotland, who had recently united the kingdoms of England and Scotland, harbored an intense fear of black magic, exacerbated by the aftermath of the Gunpowder Plot of 1605.

James I's work, Daemonologie, published in 1597, fueled this fear. It presented arguments claiming biblical proof of witchcraft, black magic, and the presence of demons on Earth, serving as a guide on spotting witches. This text is believed to have influenced William Shakespeare's works. The widespread fear of witches infiltrated all levels of society.

In this climate, two families, the Demdikes and the Chattoxs, also known as the Pendle Witches, took center stage. Led by elderly widows, Old Demdike (Elizabeth Southerns) and Old Chattox (Anne Whittle), they got by on begging and the reputation of being wise women.

The spark that ignited the Pendle Witch Trials occurred when Alizon Device, one of Demdike's granddaughters, cursed a peddler named John Law in March 1612. Though he likely suffered a stroke, the community attributed it to witchcraft, leading to Alizon's arrest and subsequent accusations against neighbors and family members.

Allegedly, a Witches Sabbat at Old Demdike's home and a plot to blow up Lancaster Castle were unveiled. Nineteen people, including the Pendle Witches and suspects from Samlesbury, spent four months in the castle dungeons, awaiting trial.

The trials began on August 18, 1612, with nine-year-old Jennet Device, a granddaughter of Demdike, as the star witness. The majority of evidence was based on rumors, hearsay, superstition, and false confessions. The accused were not allowed to call witnesses in their defense. Ten people were found guilty and hanged on Gallows Hill on August 20, 1612, for crimes like causing madness and using witchcraft to murder 16 people.

In 1616, Marie Smith, a woman from Norfolk, England, was known around her village as a glover's wife and a cheese merchant. By all accounts Marie was a normal woman who tried to scratch out a living. However, after becoming enraged when some neighbors were more successful selling cheese, Marie allegedly summoned the devil.

In a sinister encounter, the devil offered to exact revenge on those she despised if she would turn her soul over to him. Marie agreed to this unholy pact. This marked the beginning of her dark journey into witchcraft.

Driven by anger, Marie resolved to unleash malicious schemes upon those she envied. Strangely, her enemies became severely ill. One of them even developed gangrene and lost several fingers. Eventually Marie was arrested and accused of being involved in witchcraft.

As she faced the esteemed clergyman sent to decide her fate, Marie claimed to have a horned figure by her side defending her. Despite their attempts to guide her towards confession and repentance, the devil urged Marie to stay resolute in her allegiance to him, promising salvation through his dark power.

This sinister alliance led to a tragic end for Marie. As her crimes were exposed she defiantly admitted that she was a witch and would not recant her beliefs.

On January 12, 1616, Marie Smith was executed.

Jennet Device, whose testimony condemned her family in 1612, faced her own accusations of witchcraft in 1633. A ten-year-old boy named Edmund Robinson played a key role in this case, claiming he was taken to a witches' gathering. However, in November 1633, Robinson confessed to fabricating the story to avoid punishment for neglecting his chores.

The accused witches were sent to London for examination, and Charles I, skeptical of witchcraft, spared their lives. While some were pardoned, others, unable to pay for their prison stay, likely succumbed to the elements and poor conditions of the facility. The fate of Jennet Device remains uncertain, as records suggest she resided in prison until August 22, 1636. However, conflicting information raises intriguing questions about her ultimate fate and identity.

East Anglia experienced a witch fever between 1645-1646, fueled by Puritan beliefs. Matthew Hopkins, the infamous "Witchfinder General," exploited this fear, causing 68 deaths in Bury St. Edmunds and 19 in Chelmsford in a single day.

Matthew Hopkins had a particular affinity for the confessional technique known as the "swimming test." This remarkably straightforward yet potent method included securing the arms and legs of the accused to a chair and then immersing them in the village pond. The verdict was stark: if they sank and perished, they were deemed innocent and destined for heaven; however, if they floated, they would face trial as a witch.

Hopkins focused on finding a "Devil's Mark" on suspects. By finding a birthmark, a small deformity or any kind of blemish, Hopkins would use the abnormality on the skin to find guilt. Women also endured horrific torture, supervised even by James I. Methods like a "Trial by Water" which consisted of tying someone's thumb to their toe and tossing them into a lake or pond. Those who sank were vindicated in a watery grave, yet those who were able to break away and swim to safety were hunted down and executed.

Imperialism spread English witchcraft laws globally, and the colonies were no exception. Witch trials were going to be a major problem in the Massachusetts Bay Colony.

The Salem Witch Trials

Goody Glover

A few years before the Salem Witch Trials became a stain on American history, a horrible precursor to the infamous trials took place in Boston. The event centered around one woman- Goody Ann Glover.

Deported from Ireland to Barbados during Oliver Cromwell's rule, Goody (Goodwife) Ann Glover arrived in Boston as a widow in the 1680s with her daughter, facing the challenges of being a Roman Catholic in a predominantly Puritan society.

Once she got settled in the North End, Goody Glover became a housekeeper for John Goodwin. In the summer of 1688, some of Goodwin's children fell mysteriously ill. Cotton Mather, a key figure in the future Salem trials, attributed the illnesses to "hellish Witchcraft." Martha, the eldest Goodwin daughter, accused Glover after a heated argument.

Despite the lack of substantial evidence, Glover was arrested and subjected to a trial fraught with prejudice. During the proceedings, Mather called Glover "a scandalous old Irishwoman, very poor, a Roman Catholic and obstinate in idolatry." Her Gaelic testimony perplexed the court and led to her conviction. The proceedings revealed her societal marginalization as an illiterate Catholic widow who could not say the Lord's Prayer in English, amplifying the fervor against her.

The accusations gained momentum as unexplained fits afflicted the Goodwin children. Puritanical doctors, adhering to 17th-century beliefs, attributed the phenomena to witchcraft. This sparked broader attention, involving magistrates and ministers, which set the stage for the hysteria that would ultimately grip the colony.

The judges, detached from Goody's language and culture, misconstrued her words and actions, and sealed her fate. She was sentenced to death by Deputy Governor William Stoughton, who would later become an important figure in the Salem Witch Trials.

Glover was hanged in Boston on November 16, 1688. The echoes of her trial reverberated in the subsequent events in Salem, where fear, superstition, and injustice culminated in one of the darkest chapters in American colonial history.

Turmoil in Salem

In the aftermath of King William's War in 1689, the Massachusetts Bay Colony found itself grappling with an influx of refugees, straining resources and amplifying existing tensions between families in Salem. The village, led by the stringent Reverend Samuel Parris, faced a tumultuous period marked by rivalry and conflict, with the villagers attributing the chaos to the influence of the devil.

The turmoil escalated in January 1692 when Parris' 9-year-old daughter, Betty and her 11-year-old cousin, Abigail Williams, began exhibiting peculiar behavior — fits, screams, and contortions. As the strange events unfolded, a local doctor attributed the affliction to the supernatural. The contagion of hysteria soon extended to 12-year-old Ann Putnam Jr., who experienced a similar unusual outburst.

Magistrates Jonathan Corwin and John Hathorne were familiar with accusations levied by children on Goody Glover in Boston and immediately began applying pressure to the colonial officials overseeing local cases. The afflicted girls pointed fingers at three women: Tituba, a slave in the Parris household; Sarah Good, a homeless beggar; and Sarah Osborne, an impoverished elderly woman. The three accused women were brought before the magistrates for interrogation, which began on March 1, 1692.

Sarah Good

Born in 1653 to wealthy innkeeper John Solart, Sarah Good's life took a dark turn due to her father's estate litigation, leaving her virtually destitute. Her first marriage to the poor indentured servant Daniel Poole ended in 1686 with Poole's death and debts. Her second marriage to William Good was marred by financial troubles inherited from the first husband. The Goods, homeless and socially shunned, became beggars, struggling to find shelter. Sarah's unpleasant reputation contributed to their marginalization, making them a perfect target for witchcraft accusations.

On February 29, 1692, the first warrant for the arrest of Sarah Good, Sarah Osborne, and Tituba was issued, linking them to the afflictions of Betty Parris and Abigail Williams. The pregnant Sarah Good, viewed as a nuisance by many, was the first to testify in the Salem Witchcraft trials. Even her six-year-old daughter Dorcas was coerced into testifying against her. Despite her husband's ambiguous stance, Good faced overwhelming sentiment against her.

According to her teenage accuser, Elizabeth Hubbard during the witch trials, "I saw the apparition of Sarah Good, which did torture me most grievously, but I did not know her name until the 27th of February, and then she told me her name was Sarah Good, and then she did prick me and pinch me most grievously, and also since, several times, urging me vehemently to write in her (the devil's) book".

While Good never confessed, she accused Sarah Osborne of afflicting the girls during the trials. Despite attempts at defense, Judge William Stoughton did not invalidate the accusations.

Condemned to hang, Good's execution was postponed until after the birth of her child. Her daughter Dorcas, accused of witchery, suffered seven months of imprisonment, leaving her psychologically scarred.

Good's baby died in prison before her eventual hanging on July 19, 1692. Defiant until the end, Good refused to confess. She even needled Rev. Nicholas Noyes by referring to Revelation 16:6 in her last words. "You are a liar!," screamed Good. "I'm no more a witch than you are a wizard, and if you take away my life, God will give you blood to drink!"

Her words were quite prophetic. According to Salem lore, Noyes died in December 1717 from an internal hemorrhage. Like Sarah Good had predicted; he died choking on his own blood.

Sarah Osborne

Sarah Osborne, like Good, became entangled in the web of accusations during the Salem Witch Trials. Accused due to her unconventional actions, Osborne had committed fornication with her indentured servant and contested her late husband's will, breaking social norms of the time.

Her absence from church and a prolonged illness that left her bedridden painted a large target on Osborne's back. Accusations against her likely stemmed from the prominent Putnam family, with whom she was embroiled in a legal battle. Elizabeth Hubbard joined the accusers, describing Osborne's actions as pinching and poking with knitting needles.

When questioned by the magistrates, Osborne asserted her innocence and denied involvement with evil spirits or harming children, neither confessing nor accusing others.

Although she was grilled by Corwin and Hathorne, Sarah never went on trial. After spending nine weeks in jail in unsanitary conditions, Osborne died on May 10, 1692, at the age of 49.

Tituba

Born in South America before coming to Salem, Tituba, had lived a full life and knew a thing or two about a thing or two. Tituba aimed to avoid execution by demonstrating repentance, aligning with Puritan ideals. She confessed to serving the devil, narrating vivid scenes involving black dogs, red cats, yellow birds, and a "tall man with white hair" who demanded her allegiance. She detailed signing the devil's book and implicated other witches conspiring against the Puritans. Crucially, Tituba denied causing harm to the Parris children or engaging in a Satanic pact.

On March 1, in a surprising turn, Tituba confessed to witchcraft, claiming that the devil had compelled her to serve him. Aware of her vulnerable position as a slave and suspect, Tituba crafted a confession tailored to resonate with Puritan doctrine. She emphasized the innate sinfulness of women and her duty to servitude as a slave and mentioned someone that had the appearance of "a hog and sometimes like a great dog" that commanded her to hurt the children. Acknowledging Satanic involvement, Tituba invoked Scripture, emphasizing her resistance to the devil's influence.

Crucially, Tituba played into Puritan beliefs of confession and repentance leading to salvation. With a heartfelt apology, she professed her love for young Betty and expressed regret for any harm caused.

Corwin and Hathorne later paid Tituba a visit in jail and got her to admit to signing the devil's book. She also told the magistrates that she saw nine marks in the book, one for each witch in Salem. With three of them accounted for, Corwin and Hathorne were shocked to learn there were six more people in league with Satan in Salem.

Due to her cooperation and her perfect Puritan confession, a grand jury declined to indict Tituba on May 9, 1693, due to a lack of evidence. While she spent 15 months in a crowded Boston prison, Tituba escaped execution, and her case became a pivotal moment in the Salem Witch Trials.

As paranoia gripped the superstitious and devout Puritan population, a new wave of accusations from Mary Walcott, Mercy Lewis and Ann Putnam Sr would ultimately result in the death of twenty innocent people in Salem.

Bridget Bishop

As the villagers grappled with the inexplicable afflictions befalling the girls, Bridget Bishop, a widow of contentious repute, found herself ensnared in the web of accusations. Although she wasn't the first to be accused of witchcraft, Bridget was actually the first to face the gallows in a trial that would set the macabre stage for the Salem Witch Trials. Prosecutor Thomas Newton believed she would be easy to convict given her horrible reputation as she was plagued by salacious rumors and had even been accused of being a witch in Boston years earlier.

Bridget, in her third marriage to the elderly sawyer Edward Bishop, resided on the property inherited from her second husband, Thomas Oliver. Living on Washington Street in Salem Town, her life took a fateful turn when, on April 16, accusations were hurled by two of the afflicted girls.

Arrested on April 19 by Salem Marshal George Herrick, Bridget found herself at Ingersoll's Tavern in Salem Village, where she was interrogated. Denying any involvement in witchcraft, Bishop's protests fell on deaf ears. Accusers like Ann Putnam Jr. claimed, "She calls the Devil her god!" Mercy Lewis joined Putnam as a witness, and both claimed to have seen her spirit in their homes.

When Bridget's trial began, Judge Hathorne accused her of afflicting the girls, and alleged that she was responsible for her first husband's death.

Accusations against Bridget Bishop spanned years, painting a portrait of a woman steeped in the lore of witchcraft. Gossip whispered of her role in the demise of not just her first husband, but her second as well.

In 1680, she faced accusations of pinching a slave, stealing eggs, and frightening horses. Ten neighbors bolstered the claims, citing instances of her pressuring the afflicted girls to sign the Devil's book.

The trial unfolded like a grim tapestry of counter-magic, missing items, and spectral visitations. Witnesses spoke of poppets (witches' dolls) stuck with pins, disappearing spoons, money, and even seeing the accused flying through the air.

Her relationship with her second husband, Thomas Oliver, cast shadows over her reputation. Abused and bruised, Bridget's troubled marriage became a source of discomfort for the community. Accused of being equally abusive, she endured public punishment for quarrels and brawls, further alienating her from the wary villagers.

With the deck stacked against her, the jury deliberated for six days before finally deciding she was guilty of the charges. Two days later she was ordered to be executed for her crime. Sheriff George Corwin led her from the Salem jail through the streets to Gallows Hill, to the hastily built platform and secured her hands behind her back. He placed the noose around her neck and then knelt to tie her petticoats to her legs so she wouldn't become indecent as she was being hanged.

A few moments later Bridget Bishop and met her tragic end. Instead of quelling the hysteria, her death only fueled it.

The Salem Witch Trials were just getting started. However, one of the nine judges had seen enough and didn't want any part of it..

Considered to be one of the most brilliant legal minds in Massachusetts, Judge Nathaniel Saltonstall, realized he was participating in a circus. He was dissatisfied with the proceedings and resigned from the Court of Oyer and Terminer before another person could be tried in Salem.

George Burroughs

During the Salem Witch Trials anyone could be targeted as a witch, even a respected minister.

In 1680, George Burroughs arrived in Salem, seeking solace after the loss of his wife merely a year later. A man of Harvard-trained intellect, he donned the robes of a minister and began his spiritual stewardship over the village. However, the serenity of his pastoral duty was marred by a bitter dispute, a venomous clash over wages that poisoned the well of communal harmony.

This rift extended beyond matters of mere compensation. Burroughs found himself entangled in a web of personal animosity with none other than constable John Putnam, a dispute that would cast a malevolent shadow over his future.

As the echoes of discontent reverberated through the village, Burroughs abruptly departed, leaving Salem behind. Yet, the relentless fingers of fate clutched him tightly. Casco welcomed him, but Indians drove him out in 1683, compelling him to seek safety in Wells, Maine. There, amid the quietude of the landscape, he was granted 150 acres of land, a sanctuary he would later relinquish for the greater good as the population grew.

Nine years passed, and the winds of destiny swept Burroughs from the peaceful embrace of Wells into the tempest of accusation. Arrested for witchcraft on May 4, 1692, in Wells, Burroughs was ensnared by the tendrils of a complaint filed by Captain Jonathan Walcott and Thomas Putnam. Their accusations, on behalf of the afflicted girls marked the genesis of his descent into the abyss of the Salem Witch Trials.

The arrest was no ordinary affair; it unfolded under the shroud of discretion. Major Elisha Hutchinson and Field Marshal Jonathan Partridge executed the arrest with covert precision, fearing that any forewarning might allow Burroughs to escape the grasp of justice.

Upon arrival in Salem, Burroughs found himself locked in the cold confines of the town jail. His fate, however, unfolded not behind prison bars but within the suffocating atmosphere of the Salem Village meetinghouse.

On May 9, he faced the piercing scrutiny of judges John Hathorne, William Stoughton, and Jonathan Corwin, with Reverend Samuel Parris documenting the unfolding drama. Burroughs denied spectral infestations but acknowledged the presence of toads in his home in Wells. This raised red flags with the magistrates as the creatures were believed to be witches' familiars in the eyes of the superstitious.

The inquisition delved deeper, unearthing Burroughs's hazy recollections of communion and selective baptism of his children. A puritan minister mired in the fog of forgetfulness cast shadows upon his character.

Yet, the true drama unfolded during the trial on August 5, 1692. Unlike the others who had been put on trial, Burroughs had studied at Harvard and knew a little about the law. He knew what the magistrates were required to do, and he knew he was within his rights to have some jurors removed that he believed were going to be less favorable to him. However, unlike the others before him, Burroughs stood accused not merely of witchcraft but of leading a coven. According to his accusers, Satan had promised him that he would one day be the King of Hell. The notion that the Devil could infiltrate the sanctum of the church sent shivers through the hearts of the fearful Salem people.

Burroughs faced a barrage of accusations from a multitude of witnesses. Thirty voices wove a tapestry of tales, painting him as a witch and, more ominously, a leader of witches. Rumors of magical superhuman strength resonated through the testimonies, with witnesses recounting Burroughs's claims of lifting a seven-pound musket by sticking his fingers into the barrel and lifting heavy barrels of cider single-handedly.

His secretive nature, a recurring theme, surfaced in tales of attempts to silence his former wives. The courtroom buzzed with the inexplicable, and Burroughs's fate hung in the balance.

Oddly, the testimonies of the afflicted girls bore an eerie similarity, raising suspicions of manipulation by figures like Thomas Putnam. The language mirrored one another, hinting at a scripted narrative designed to strengthen the case against Burroughs.

Despite physical examinations revealing "nothing upon the body of the above-said Burroughs but what is natural," his time was up. On August 19, 1692, George Burroughs, alongside other convicted witches George Jacobs, John Proctor, John Willard, and Martha Carrier, ascended the scaffold at Proctor's Ledge.

Burroughs, standing atop the precipice of death, delivered an eloquent speech proclaiming his innocence. With a big booming voice, he recited the Lord's prayer flawlessly, defying the belief that witches stumbled over sacred words. The crowd stirred, and whispers of dissent wafted through the air.

But Burroughs had been sentenced to die and the powers that be were not swayed by the last minute of groundswell support for the minister. The executioner's hand released the platform, and his body swung in a macabre dance.

A heatwave compelled immediate burial in a shallow grave at the execution site. Burroughs, stripped of his clothing and dignity, joined Willard and Carrier in an unmarked tomb, his chin and foot left exposed by the shallow earth.

The fate of his body after that fateful day at Proctor's Ledge eludes historical records.

Rebecca Nurse

Rebecca Nurse was an almost deaf 71-year-old grandmother and the wife of a respected artist. She was an unlikely target for the storm that brewed on the horizon. On March 24, 1692, the news of her arrest reverberated through Salem. To many, Nurse epitomized piety and virtue, a beloved figure in the community. Her unexpected fall from grace came as a shock, a ripple through the collective conscience of Salem.

The accusations, spearheaded by Ann Putnam, Jr., Ann Putnam, Sr., and Abigail Williams, pierced the veil of Nurse's revered reputation. Her unabashed criticism of the accusers, particularly Ann Putnam, Jr., Ann Putnam, Sr., and Abigail Williams, served as the catalyst for the malevolent accusations that followed. In a society where dissent and outspokenness were perilous, Nurse found herself ensnared in the web of suspicion.

Reverend Deodat Lawson of Boston, an accuser with purported spiritual insight, claimed to witness Nurse's spectral form tormenting Ann Putnam, Sr., in her own home. The stage was set, and the trial unfurled, painting Nurse as a malevolent force haunting the accusers.

During her examination on March 24, Nurse, with unwavering conviction, proclaimed her innocence. In the courtroom, she declared before her Eternal Father, "I am innocent, and God will clear my innocency... The Lord knows I have not hurt them. I am an innocent person." Her words, a plea to divine justice, echoed through the room. Unlike others who were charged with being a witch, Nurse brought in witnesses that called the accuser's character into question.

As the trial unfolded in June 1692, the jury, swayed by Nurse's well-established reputation and the support of 39 individuals who risked their own safety to sign a petition in her favor, pronounced a verdict of "not guilty." Salem, for a fleeting moment, tasted the bittersweetness of justice finally being served.

Yet, the capricious winds of hysteria were not easily quelled. As the words "not guilty" reverberated in the courtroom, a discordant symphony erupted. The afflicted girls convulsed in fits and writhed in agony in front of everyone. In the aftermath of this strange spectacle, the once steadfast jury succumbed to the pressure, altering their decision to a damning "guilty."

On July 19, 1692, the sentence loomed over Rebecca Nurse like a specter. The once-revered matriarch of Salem was hanged. According to legend, her son, Benjamin, clandestinely rowed a boat under the shroud of night to claim his mother's body, ensuring a Christian burial on the sacred grounds of home.

Rebecca Nurse's conviction and subsequent execution marked a turning point in the Salem Witch Trials. The citizens, once resolute in their belief, now questioned the credibility of accusations leveled against seemingly pious individuals. Doubt permeated the collective consciousness, and the seeds of skepticism were sown.

Alice Parker

Alice Parker lived a quiet but increasingly scrutinized life. Married to John Parker, a humble fisherman, Alice found herself ensnared in the web of hysteria that characterized the Salem Witch Trials.

Alice's troubles began in the spring of 1692, when Mary Warren, one of the afflicted girls, claimed that Alice's specter had visited her in the night, tormenting her with pinches and strangling sensations. The community, already on edge from months of accusations and trials, was quick to believe these spectral encounters as irrefutable evidence of witchcraft. As the allegations against Alice mounted, so did the pressure on her.

On May 12, 1692, Alice Parker was brought before the magistrates for examination. The atmosphere in the courtroom was tense. As Alice stood before her accuser, Mary Warren, she vehemently denied the charges of witchcraft. In fact, she claimed to have never even spoken to Mary. However, her denials were drowned out by Mary Warren falling onto the floor as she went into a seizure. Margaret Jacobs also cast aspersions on Alice, describing vivid encounters with Alice's specter, painting her as a malevolent presence that sought to harm them in the dead of night.

Among the witnesses was William Beale, who testified that he had seen Alice at a witchcraft meeting. His testimony, though lacking physical evidence, was enough to sway the court. The spectral evidence, which consisted of the afflicted girls' visions and experiences, played a significant role in the proceedings. This type of evidence, though controversial and later discredited, was considered legitimate at the time and sealed Alice's fate.

Despite her pleas of innocence, Alice Parker was found guilty of witchcraft. The court, influenced by the mass hysteria and the persuasive, albeit intangible, testimonies, sentenced her to death. Alice's execution was scheduled for September 22, 1692.

On the day of her execution, Alice Parker was carried to Gallows Hill in a wagon with seven others that were to be executed. The somber procession was a stark reminder of the fear that had taken hold of Salem. Strangely, the cart got stuck in the mud as is approached the execution site, and according to Salem lore, the afflicted girls claimed to see the devil holding onto the wagon, desperately trying to pull it back into the village.

Eventually, a group of men got the wagon moving again and the group made their way to the execution site. Alice maintained her innocence to the very end. Her execution was swift, and her body, like those of the other convicted witches, was buried in an unmarked grave.

Martha and Giles Corey

Like many others in Salem, Martha Corey and her husband Giles found themselves ensnared in a web of accusations that would lead to tragedy.

Martha, a woman who proudly proclaimed herself a "Gospel woman" since her acceptance into the church, faced an uncertain fate when the accusations of witchcraft descended upon her. The exact reasons for her being targeted remain unclear. Speculations hinted at gossip, the perceived attempt to dissuade her husband from attending the examinations, or Giles's own public complaints about his wife. Whatever the catalyst, the wheels of suspicion had begun to turn.

By March 21, Martha Corey was under arrest, defiantly maintaining her innocence even as the afflicted girls contorted in agony. Her bold laughter at their antics and a demand to deliver an opening prayer had everyone buzzing. As the accusations mounted, Martha went on trial and her every word was scrutinized.

Giles Corey, her husband, was a scoundrel who was known to be an arsonist and someone who had a propensity for violence. As he entered his trial, he entered the narrative with a complex role. Questioned about odd occurrences at their home, including the unexplained sicknesses of an ox and a cat, Giles found himself in a precarious position. He criticized Martha and hinted at possessing knowledge that could "fix her business."

On April 18, an official complaint was lodged against Giles, leading to his arrest. The old couple, seemingly trapped in a vortex of accusations, faced the tumultuous proceedings of the court.

As September approached, the specters of both Coreys continued to haunt the accusers. Giles, scheduled for trial, refused to comply with the expected "By God and my country" declaration. Sensing an impending unjust fate, he chose to stand mute, a resolute act of defiance against a court he deemed prejudiced.

Martha faced the court's judgment and was indicted, eventually meeting her tragic end on September 22. She was hanged on Proctor's Ledge at Gallows Hill. Giles Corey, however, confronted a more harrowing fate.

The court resorted to the archaic and illegal practice of *peine forte et dure*. Giles was taken to an empty field near the Salem jail and stripped of his clothes. He was then ordered to lay on the ground and a large board was placed over him. Sheriff Corwin then began placing heavy rocks on top of him. Demanding a plea from Giles, Corwin continued to add stones. At one point he even climbed onto the board as well.

Giles, steadfast in his silence, endured this torturous ordeal. As Corwin continued to apply more large rocks, the accused warlock yelled, "More Weight!" As he slowly died from the pressure, Giles' tongue was pressed from his mouth as he struggled for air. Sheriff Corwin coldly pushed it back into Giles' mouth with his cane as he took his final breaths and finally succumbed to the weight of the stones.

Giles' body, denied a Christian burial, found a resting place near Tapley's Brook.

The End

As the tumultuous chapter of the Salem Witch Trials drew to a close, its tendrils extended into Andover, Massachusetts, ensnaring over 40 citizens, predominantly women and children. The legal proceedings cast a shadow over the town, leading to the convictions and executions of three residents: Martha Carrier, Mary Ayer Parker, and Samuel Wardwell. Ann Foster passed away in prison. Additionally, five others either pleaded guilty during arraignment or were convicted at trial.

Andover, gripped by hysteria, witnessed the involvement of 80% of its residents in the witch hunt. The town earned the dubious distinction of harboring the highest number of confessed witches and the greatest number of arrested children. As the madness ensued, a dog accused of bewitching a young girl was shot on site by bloodthirsty villagers.

Over in Salem, on September 22, 1692, the final eight individuals faced execution, marking the conclusion of the Salem Witch Trials' hangings.

On October 29, shortly after his wife had been accused of being a witch, Governor Phips dissolved the Court of Oyer and Terminer, initiating a new phase of legal proceedings. The remaining 52 individuals in jail faced trial in the Superior Court of Judicature during the subsequent winter. This new court saw a shift in the standards of evidence. Increase Mather, a prominent Boston minister and father of Cotton Mather, took a stand against the use of spectral evidence in October 1692, emphasizing the importance of preserving innocence. Once spectral evidence was excluded, many of the accused were found not guilty or released due to a lack of substantial proof.

Governor Phips, responding to the shifting dynamics and mounting public discontent, intervened to pardon those found guilty. The final prisoners were released in May 1693, bringing an end to a dark and regrettable chapter in colonial American history.

However, the repercussions of the trials were profound. Nineteen individuals had been hanged on Gallows Hill, and Giles Corey, faced a gruesome death by pressing after refusing trial. At least five accused witches perished in jail.

As the years unfolded after the haunting conclusion of the Salem Witch Trials, the inhabitants of the Massachusetts colony found themselves burdened with shame and remorse for the grievous errors that had transpired. The aftermath of the trials cast a lingering shadow, manifesting in a series of misfortunes that befell the community. Droughts, crop failures, smallpox outbreaks, and Native-American attacks plagued the once-thriving colony, prompting whispers among the populace that divine retribution was exacting its toll for the grave mistake committed during the witch trials.

The Aftermath

In a notable attempt at reconciliation with a higher power, Governor William Stoughton issued a proclamation on December 17, 1697. The proclamation called for a Day of Prayer with Fasting throughout the Province, urging all God's people to seek forgiveness for the sins that had provoked divine jealousy. The aim was to humbly acknowledge the errors committed during the trials, beseeching God for mercy and guidance to prevent a recurrence of such tragic events.

The Day of Official Repentance took place on January 15, 1697, marking a collective effort to atone for the sins that had tainted the colony. Judge Samuel Sewall, a prominent figure in the trials, attended prayer services at Boston's South Church. On this solemn occasion, Sewall requested Reverend Samuel Willard to read a public apology he had penned, accepting blame for the tragedy and seeking pardon from God and fellow men.

The healing process extended beyond individual remorse. Afflicted girl Ann Putnam, Jr., who had played a role in accusing innocent individuals, issued a poignant public apology in 1706. She expressed deep remorse for her actions, acknowledging the delusion that had led her to accuse innocent neighbors. Ann Putnam, Jr. sought forgiveness and laid bare the extent of her regret, particularly in the case of her neighbor Rebecca Nurse.

In 1711, the colony took a significant step toward rectification by passing a bill that restored the names of some convicted witches and allocated £600 in restitution to their heirs. Notably, the bill cleared the names of those who had suffered unjustly, including George Burroughs, John Proctor, Rebecca Nurse, Giles Corey, and others. However, due to the wishes of some families, not all victims were named in the restitution.

The legal exoneration extended to law enforcement involved in the trials, shielding them from prosecution for actions taken in the execution of their duties. Yet, the scars of the trials lingered, affecting the families of the victims, who had endured unimaginable suffering.

In 1957, the state of Massachusetts formally apologized for the Salem Witch Trials and cleared the names of some remaining victims. However, this apology did not extend to all victims, with Bridget Bishop and certain others left unnamed.

The quest for justice continued in 2001 when the state amended the 1957 apology, clearing the names of the remaining unnamed victims, including Ann Pudeator, Bridget Bishop, Susannah Martin, Alice Parker, Margaret Scott, and Wilmot Redd. This official acknowledgment sought to rectify the historical record and provide a measure of closure to the descendants of those wrongly accused.

The Salem Witch Trials Memorial, unveiled on August 5, 1992, marked the 300th anniversary of the trials. Nobel Laureate Elie Wiesel dedicated the memorial, designed by James Cutler and Maggie Smith.

It features a three-sided granite wall with benches, displaying the names and execution dates of each victim. Inscriptions on the ground near the entrance bear the victims' pleas of innocence, symbolizing the indifference to oppression in 1692.

In 2016, the site where the hangings took place was officially identified as Proctor's Ledge, and in 2017, a memorial designed by landscape architect Martha Lyons was unveiled at the base of the ledge to commemorate the 325th anniversary of the Salem Witch Trials.

The ceremony served as a poignant reminder of the dark chapter in history and a testament to the enduring commitment to remember and learn from the tragic events of the past.

Today Salem, Massachusetts is thriving and has become a premier tourist destination for wiccans, Halloween enthusiasts and history buffs.

The Salem Witch Trials Return

Lost in the shadow of the 1692 Witch Trials was a lesser-known witch trial in 1878 that also took place in Salem, Massachusetts. This time, the defendant was Daniel Spofford, a Newburyport resident and an early follower of Mary Baker Eddy, the founder of the Christian Science movement. The accuser was Lucretia Brown, an invalid living in Salem who had become a disciple of Eddy.

Daniel Spofford's journey to this trial began in his earlier years. Born in New Hampshire, he grew up as a menial laborer and later became a watchmaker's apprentice in eastern Massachusetts. At the age of 19, he enlisted in the United States Army and served in the American Civil War. Post-war, he worked in a shoemaker's shop in Lynn, Massachusetts, and around 1867, obtained copies of some of Mary Baker Glover's early writings on Christian Science.

Lucretia Brown, who had been an invalid since a spine injury in her childhood, experienced a 'relapse' in 1875. She had become a devoted follower of Mary Baker Eddy's teachings and was convinced that Christian Science had healed her. However, her beliefs took a dark turn when she became convinced that Daniel Spofford was afflicting her with malevolent powers and causing her poor health. Encouraged by Eddy, who believed Spofford was an enemy of her church, Brown decided to take legal action against him.

Mary Baker Eddy

Eddy, fervently convinced of Spofford's malevolence, made a determined effort to publicly prosecute him for alleged witchcraft. Despite Brown's lawyer refusing to argue the case in court, Eddy appointed one of her students, Edward Arens, to represent the case. She also gathered twenty of her followers as witnesses, although some protested and claimed that they knew nothing about the case.

On June 3, 1875, Eddy's entourage arrived at the courthouse in Salem. However, Spofford did not bother to show up in court to face the allegations. When Arens presented the complaint before Judge Horace Gray, Spofford's attorney objected, arguing that the court had no power to control his client's mind. Judge Gray concurred, dismissing the case due to "defects in the writ." The judge didn't permit Eddy to argue her view that disease could be caused by mesmeric powers.

The case, which might likely be the last witchcraft charge in the United States, was abruptly thrown out of court in the town that had witnessed the infamous Salem witch trials nearly 200 years prior. Eddy failed to convince the court of Spofford's alleged "witchcraft," but the trial illustrated how beliefs in supernatural evils persisted even into the late 19th century.

This bizarre sequel, overlooked in the shadow of the Salem Witch Trials, marked the final chapter of over two centuries of witch hunting in America. Despite its historical significance, it has been largely forgotten, serving as a strange footnote to the era of witchcraft trials in the United States.

Other Witch Trials

America's First Witch

In the early years of the Virginia colony, during the unsettling times of the 1620s, accusations of witchcraft reached the Virginia General Court, bringing forth the case of Joan Wright. In a time when Massachusetts was infamous for stoning and hanging witches, Virginia took a more moderate approach.

Joan Wright, a midwife residing in lower James City County (now Surry County), found herself accused of witchcraft in 1626. Lieutenant Giles Allington emerged as the primary witness against her, recounting a series of misfortunes that he believed were brought about by Joan's alleged sorcery. According to Allington, Joan, who was left-handed, tended to his wife during pregnancy, causing distress to his family. Disturbed by the idea of a left-handed midwife, Allington's wife insisted on securing the services of another midwife.

Following the birth of their child, Allington's wife experienced soreness in her breast, and Allington himself fell seriously ill. Tragically, their newborn, after a period of illness, passed away. In the eyes of Allington and the court, Joan Wright became the scapegoat for these misfortunes.

Additional witnesses, including a man named Booth, came forward with claims of being crossed by a woman, rendering them unable to shoot any game for an entire year. Rebecca Graye testified that Joan had predicted her husband's imminent death, with similar warnings given to others. Several witnesses attested to Joan's alleged threats against servants and acts of property destruction. One farmer even alleged that she caused a downpour that ruined his entire crop of tobacco.

Isabel Perry, another participant in Joan's trial, testified that Joan "was already well acquainted with the works of the Prince of Darkness before she left England for Virginia." This statement added a layer of suspicion to Joan's alleged activities, suggesting a pre-existing association with dark forces.

The court, led by Governor Sir George Yeardley, faced the task of determining Joan Wright's guilt or innocence. Her husband, questioned about her conduct, could only assert his ignorance of any crimes committed by his wife during their sixteen-year marriage.

When asked why she did not complain to the court, since the accusations against her were not true Joan replied, "God forgive them, and so made light of it."

Unfortunately, the records of Virginia's criminal court from this period were lost during the Civil War, leaving the fate of Joan Wright undocumented. While the historical records provide a glimpse into the witchcraft beliefs and accusations of the time, the true story of Joan Wright remains shrouded in mystery. It's highly unlikely that she was a malicious agent of the Devil.

Sadly, she was an unfortunate victim caught in the hysteria of a tragic chapter in American history. However, lost in all the madness is that fact that Joan Wright was America's first documented "witch."

The Devil & Mary Johnson

In the 17th century Mary Johnson found herself entangled in a tale of fear, suspicion, and eventual persecution in Hartford, Connecticut. She was a widow known for her expertise in herbal remedies, which had previously garnered respect in her community. However, when a series of unexplained illnesses befell the town, sparking anxiety and whispers of supernatural influences, her knowledge of herbs became a source of unease.

Under the fervent guidance of Reverend Samuel Stone's sermons and amidst the growing atmosphere of fear, accusations of witchcraft began to swirl. Mary, unfortunately, found herself at the center of these suspicions. Her arrest and subsequent interrogations took place in this climate of hysteria, where the fundamental belief in witchcraft overshadowed rationality and justice.

Under immense pressure, Mary confessed to practicing dark arts. Mary Johnson's confessions were troubling. She claimed to possess the ability to compel the Devil to assist her in daily tasks like removing fireplace ashes and managing hogs, a confounding and surreal aspect given the nature of her alleged 'dealings' with the Devil. Other admissions while in jail included heinous crimes such as murdering a child and engaging in acts of "uncleanness" with men and even devils. It's peculiar that murder was not a part of her indictment, leading to speculation about the true nature of her confession.

Under the pressure and perhaps duress of the times, Mary's confession of witchcraft led to her being found guilty of "familiarity with the devil" in December 1648.

However, since Mary was pregnant, her execution was delayed for eighteen months. After giving birth to a son while in confinement, she was hanged in June 1650.

The Hartford Witch Panic

In 1662, Hartford experienced another witch panic that was more widespread. Aside from one case during this time, there is little record of what exactly happened when twelve people were accused of witchcraft in Hartford. This period, known as the Hartford Witch Panic, resulted in the execution of four individuals.

The panic was triggered when eight-year-old Elizabeth Kelly became mysteriously ill. This led her to accuse a neighbor, Judith "Goody" Ayres, of causing her suffering through witchcraft. Before she died, Elizabeth's chilling last words set off a wave of fear and suspicion. "Father, father", the child cried. "Help me! Goodwife Ayres is upon me. She chokes me. She kneels on my belly. She will break my bowels. She pinches me. She will make me black and blue. Goodwife Ayres torments me, she pricks me with pins. She will kill me! Oh Father, set on the great furnace and scald her, get the broad ax and cut off her head!"

When Elizabeth finally died, Ayres was summoned to the home and ordered to sit next to the girl as she was grilled by authorities. Elizabeth's sleeves were rolled up revealing that she had bruises on her arms and shoulders. Strangely, as Ayres sat there a large red spot appeared on the dead girl's cheek.

After an examination it was determined that Elizabeth Kelly had not died of natural causes and that she had suffered unnatural harm. Goody Ayres was not accused of murder, but it was all but implied that she somehow had a hand in it by using witchcraft. In fact, her neighbor, Goodwife Burr testified that Ayres had encounters with the devil in England before coming to Connecticut.

Faced with the threat of execution, Elizabeth Ayres and her husband chose to flee Hartford, abandoning their eight-year-old son as well as their home and possessions. Several months later, the child was placed in a home with a cooper to serve as an apprentice. The Ayres were never seen again in Connecticut.

Around the same time, Ann Cole, a deeply religious woman from Hartford, began experiencing fits and speaking in strange voices, which were interpreted as signs of "diabolical possession". These episodes took place in her home as well as in the church. During one of the bouts, Ann fell to the floor and began convulsing. The scene was so intense that it caused one member of the congregation to faint. During some of these fits Ann began to speak English with a Dutch accent which many thought was unusual. As she was facing accusations of being a witch, Ann began naming others in the community such as Nathaniel and Rebecca Greensmith. Coincidentally, after she started pointing her finger at others, Ann stopped having the episodes and went about living a normal life.

However, the Greensmiths that had been accused by Ann didn't get off so easily. They made confessions under duress implicating others in the community.

Under intense pressure and likely torture, Rebecca confessed to being a witch and implicated her husband and several others in her confession. Her statements were detailed and vivid, describing meetings with the devil and other witches in the woods, where they allegedly plotted malevolent acts against their neighbors.

Rebecca's confession included tales of her dissatisfaction with her husband and her belief that the devil would offer her a better life. She also spoke of enchanted cakes and magical herbs, which she claimed to have used in her witchcraft practices. This confession was typical of the time, where confessions often included elaborate and fantastical elements, likely influenced by the interrogators' leading questions and the accused's desperate circumstances.

The trial was swift. Nathaniel and Rebecca Greensmith were found guilty of entertaining familiarity with Satan and sentenced to death. They were executed by hanging on January 25, 1663.

Mary Barnes, a married mother of four in nearby Farmington was another notable victim of the hysteria. Not being a member of her church likely made her an easy target. She was arrested in January 1663, and her trial quickly led to her execution on the same day as the Greensmiths.

Judith Varlet, Katherine Palmer, and James Wakely were also caught up in the frenzy, though they managed to escape execution. Varlet's and Wakely's fates remain somewhat cloudy, but Palmer is believed to have fled to Rhode Island to avoid prosecution.

John and Elizabeth Blackleach were also accused of using witchcraft. However, they were proactive in their defense, and filed slander charges against those who had accused them. Naturally, the charges against them went away.

Andrew Sanford was also accused of being a witch. Not long after, his wife, Mary was also indicted. Strangely, when they had their day in court, Andrew was acquitted, yet Mary was found guilty. While there is no record of Mary's execution, it is believed that she soon met her Maker at the end of a rope like too many others during this time. Mary Sanford was the last person hanged in the Hartford Witch Panic of 1662.

After traveling to London, Connecticut Governor John Winthrop returned home and used his authority to reform the legal proceedings related to witchcraft. Winthrop was not in favor of the spectral evidence that had been commonly used to convict accused witches. With his steady hand leading the colony, the temperature was turned down, for a while…

More Trouble in Connecticut

Five years after the hangings in Hartford, just six miles away in the town of Wethersfield, witch trials returned to Connecticut. Katherine Harrison, a woman who was once a servant in Hartford became a wealthy widow after her husband, John mysteriously died. Her inheritance, valued at nearly a thousand pounds, made her one of the wealthiest women in the colony. This sudden shift in status was a rare occurrence, especially for women, and it set her apart from those in the community.

In 1668, people began to whisper that Katherine was a self-professed fortune teller who possessed supernatural powers and used them to harm others. Katherine's practice of medicine and her knowledge of herbal remedies, which she used to help those in need, became twisted into evidence of her involvement in witchcraft.

Katherine Harrison's trial the following year was a pivotal moment in the history of witchcraft prosecutions in Connecticut. The court proceedings relied heavily on spectral evidence and testimonies from her neighbors, who accused her of various forms of maleficium (harmful magic). Over 30 witnesses testified against her, recounting instances of fortune-telling, sightings of her ghostly apparition, and allegations that she had caused illnesses and deaths. Neighbors and accusers often alleged that the witches' supernatural powers extended to their animals and crops, and any misfortune or strange behavior in livestock could be interpreted as a sign of witchcraft.

One particularly damning piece of evidence was a testimony that Katherine had spun an unusually large quantity of fine linen yarn, an act deemed suspiciously beyond normal human capability. Her ability to produce such an abundance of yarn was interpreted as a sign of supernatural assistance. Moreover, her practice of medicine raised further suspicions, with former patients claiming that her treatments were responsible for their ailments rather than cures.

In 1670 she was found guilty and sentenced to death. However, due to pressure applied by Governor John Winthrop who was skeptical of the claims against Katherine, she was forced to pay a fine and essentially banished from the community.

After her banishment, Katherine had to find a new place to live. Records indicate she relocated to Westchester, New York, but establishing herself in a new community proved to be challenging, particularly with the stigma of her witchcraft conviction hanging over her. After run-ins with neighbors that resulted in various lawsuits, Katherine quietly moved back to Connecticut and lived the rest of her life.

Grace Sherwood

Born to carpenter John White and his wife Susan in the quiet farming community of Pungo, Virginia, Grace White was a tall, slender, and captivatingly beautiful woman who turned many heads. She married James Sherwood and settled down on a farm in the area where she became the mother of three boys. However, Grace's life took a dark turn when she found herself in the crosshairs of neighbors who didn't like the attractive lady who made strange concoctions with herbs grown on her farm.

Accusations began in 1697 when a neighbor named Richard Capps accused Grace of enchanting his bull and causing it to die. Nothing came of the accusations but a short time later another villager, John Gisburn accused Grace of being a witch and killing his cotton crop with sorcery. Incensed by these claims, Grace and her husband took legal action, suing Gisburn for slander. The legal turmoil continued when another neighbor, Elizabeth Barnes, alleged Grace assumed the form of a cat and broke into her house and assaulted her.

In retaliation, Grace sued Elizabeth for slander. The legal wrangling escalated when, after the death of her husband James in 1701, Grace and Elizabeth Barnes got into a physical confrontation. Elizabeth got the best of Grace. Battered and bruised, Grace sued Elizabeth for assault. The courts sided with the attractive widow once again, this time awarding her twenty shillings.

Furious over the decision and lacking the means to pay, Elizabeth and her husband resorted to a drastic measure. In a desperate attempt to shift the narrative, they accused Grace of being a witch before a magistrate. The stage was set for a dramatic turn of events.

On January 3, 1706, she was ordered to appear in court on charges of witchcraft. However, she neither answered the charge nor showed up for the court hearing. Authorities, suspecting an unholy relationship with the devil, searched Grace's house for evidence but found nothing conclusive.

In an attempt to prove her guilt or innocence, the court ordered Grace to be observed by a group of her peers – 12 local women. A thorough examination revealed two strange warts on her body, believed to be marks of the devil. The justice ordered a second examination but finding 12 different women in her village proved difficult. In the absence of the required second inspection, Grace was subjected to a "witch ducking".

On the fateful day, bound with her hands to her feet and a millstone tied around her neck, Grace was thrown from a small boat into the Lynnhaven River at a place known as "Witch's Duck Point". If she were a witch, she would swim away, but if innocent, she would face the vindication of a watery grave.

As the millstone was being placed around her neck, Grace cried out, "I be not a witch, I be a healer!"

Although she initially started to sink, Grace managed to untie herself and swim away. Strangely, when the sheriff grabbed her, a violent storm blew out of nowhere and a torrential downpour ensued.

Since she survived the "Trial by Water" Grace Sherwood spent seven years in jail as punishment for the accusations of witchcraft. After her release, she returned to her home and lived peacefully until her death at the age of eighty. According to legend, Grace tried to flee

Virginia and sail to England but was never able to find anyone who was willing to carry a convicted witch across the Atlantic Ocean. It was said that after her death Grace's children placed her body in front of the fireplace. Within moments a violent wind swept through the house and when it stopped all that was left was a pile of ashes in the floor with a cloven footprint stamped in the middle of it.

While it's not very likely that the devil came to claim Grace's body, it is a tale that has been passed down for generations in Princess Anne County.

Three hundred years later after the infamous Trial by Water, on July 10, 2006, Virginia Governor Tim Kaine pardoned Grace Sherwood and restored her good name. The so-called "Witch of Pungo" was finally vindicated.

On April 21, 2007, a statue immortalizing Grace Sherwood was erected in Virginia Beach, near the very spot where she faced the infamous ducking.

Goody Cole

In the small town of Hampton, New Hampshire, a shadowy tale of injustice and superstition unfolded in the 17th century, centered around a woman known as Eunice "Goody" Cole. Goody Cole was the only person ever found guilty of witchcraft in the state of New Hampshire.

Goody Cole's ordeal began in 1656 when she was accused of witchcraft by her own neighbors. She was subjected to a trial, which, in the fervor of the times, led to her conviction. She was imprisoned in Boston but was eventually released several years later due to her deteriorating health. Goody Cole returned to her hometown of Hampton, where she was assigned a meager hut in which to live out her days. The people of Hampton, however, did not welcome her back with open arms. The specter of witchcraft still hung over her, and many believed that she had made a sinister pact with the devil.

Her life in Hampton was marked by isolation, disdain, and a palpable sense of dread from her fellow townspeople. But Goody Cole's story did not end there.

In 1673, she faced another trial, this time found not guilty of the witchcraft accusations. Centuries later, in 1938, a society called "The Society in Hampton for the Apprehension of Those Falsely Accusing Eunice 'Goody' Cole of Having Familiarity with the Devil" emerged. This society was dedicated to clearing her name and rectifying the injustices done to her. During a public ceremony in 1938, Goody Cole's citizenship was posthumously restored. Certified copies of her court documents were ceremoniously burned, and the ashes, combined with soil from her last residence, were intended for burial. However, they eventually found their way to the Tuck Museum, a local historical institution, where they are now preserved.

In 1963, a memorial to Goody Cole was established on the site believed to be her former property, a testament to the ongoing efforts to exonerate her. Harold Fernald, a Hampton resident and a teacher, created this unmarked sculpted boulder on the historic town green as a somber tribute to Goody Cole's tragic life.

The Witch of Ridley Creek

In 1684, in the lands that would eventually become Chester County, Pennsylvania, an unusual event unfolded, marking the inception of the only official witch trial in the state's history. The catalyst for this extraordinary trial was a crisis involving Henry Drystreet, who noticed that his cows had mysteriously stopped producing milk. Suspicion quickly turned to the mysterious figure of Margaret Mattson; a Swedish woman rumored to possess the powers of a witch by many in the local community.

Margaret and her husband Neels were among the Swedish-Finnish settlers living in the New Sweden area near Ridley Creek in Eddystone, Pennsylvania. The accusations against Margaret were grounded in the belief that she had bewitched Drystreet's livestock and caused his misfortune.

During the 1680s, the practice of witchcraft was taken very seriously, as evidenced by the infamous Salem witch trials in Massachusetts, which occurred a decade later. Pennsylvania's situation could have spiraled into a similar frenzy, but a key figure made a significant difference. The colony's founder, William Penn, personally presided over Margaret Mattson's case, ensuring that she received a fair and just trial.

Margaret, who spoke Swedish, was provided with an interpreter to ensure she could effectively defend herself. Furthermore, the jury was composed of fellow Swedes, showcasing a progressive approach for the time. This was a notable departure from the norms in England, where women were not allowed to testify in criminal cases until the 19th century.

One crucial aspect of this trial was that it did not involve the death penalty. William Penn had abolished the death penalty for all crimes except willful murder in Pennsylvania. However, this was to change in 1718 when witchcraft became one of the 14 capital offenses in the state.

William Penn

The trial itself was marred by questionable testimonies and hearsay. Witnesses relied on vague accounts and hearsay, with charges ranging from witchcraft against animals to fantastic stories of Margaret appearing at the foot of someone's bed, threatening to send their cows to hell. The first person to testify was the angry neighbor, Henry Drystreet. Drystreet told the jury that he had been told twenty years earlier, that Margaret was a witch and that she had cast spells on some cows. When prodded, Henry was not sure who the cows belonged to, but he was certain that she was a witch all the same.

Charles Ashcom, another villager told of a conversation he had with Margaret's daughter. According to the young lady, her mother had used sorcery to bewitch her cattle and she was forced to sell them.

Other neighbors also testified about strange happenings with Margaret that left them unsettled.

Throughout the trial, Margaret Mattson consistently denied all allegations and at one point asked where her daughter was and invited her to come speak. "Where is my daughter," asked Margaret. "Let her come and say so!"

The accused witch was clearly angry and denied all the charges, asserting that the witnesses spoke solely based on hearsay. However, during that era, hearsay testimony was considered admissible. When the jury foreman John Hastings read the verdict in the courtroom, you could have heard a pin drop.

"We find Margaret Mattson guilty of having common fame of a witch, but not guilty in the manner and form as she stands indicted."

In modern terms, she was ultimately found guilty of having the reputation of a witch but not guilty of actual witchcraft.

This verdict allowed William Penn to uphold his Quaker values and commitment to tolerance. Under his authority, no one accused of witchcraft was executed, and official laws against witchcraft were not established in Pennsylvania until long after his passing.

In the case of "The Witch of Ridley Creek", there was a unique form of punishment imposed. A fine of 50 pounds was levied on the husband of the accused women as a "peace bond." If no further charges were brought against the women in the following six months, the money would be returned. This practice was common among Quakers and served as a guarantee of good behavior. Margaret Mattson' husband and son in law each put up fifty pounds as a guarantee that she would stay out of trouble for six months. Once the bond was secured, she was allowed to return home.

Margaret had no further issues and her family got their money back.

The Fairfield County Witch Trials

In 1792, in the heart of Fairfield County, South Carolina, a shadow of fear descended upon the peaceful town of Winnsboro. It all began with the inexplicable plague that befell the cattle, causing many cows to die. Strange occurrences soon followed, as residents of the town exhibited bizarre behavior, claiming to be possessed by unseen forces. With no rational explanation for the sudden loss of cattle and the peculiar conduct of their neighbors, whispers of witchcraft began to permeate the community.

Amidst the growing unease, four individuals found themselves accused of being witches, though the majority of the accusations pointed fingers at a woman named Mary Ingleman.

Witnesses testified to her wielding supernatural powers, describing how she had used magic to lift a cow and cruelly slam it back to the ground, resulting in a broken neck. Others claimed she had cast spells that allowed her to levitate people off the ground or transform into various animals, including a menacing black panther.

Yet, one accusation surpassed them all in its absurdity: the claim that Mary Ingleman had transformed a young man into a horse and ridden him to a witches' gathering where even the devil himself was said to be in attendance. The townsfolk, desperate to find an explanation for their misfortunes and keen to avoid the mass hysteria that had plagued the Salem Witch trials, hastily turned their ire toward Mary Ingleman and her three neighbors.

Without concrete evidence, these accused individuals were subjected to a makeshift trial held at a local farm, where a single man assumed the roles of both judge and jury. The accused were subjected to beatings, torture, and the threat of burning, nearly pushed to the brink of death.

According to South Carolina lore, Mary Ingleman was even hanged but somehow she used her powers to survive and was cut down from the gallows. However, father time would eventually come calling. Mary eventually succumbed to old age.

"If the Bible is Heavier..."

In the year 1805, in the seemingly tranquil town of Bethel, Ohio, a dark cloud of superstition and fear descended upon its residents. This is the tale of the Bethel Witch Trial, a peculiar chapter in American history.

The story began with the Hildebrand family, whose daughters exhibited bizarre behavior. The girls, now young women, were seemingly possessed by malevolent spirits. They would scream at night, terrified by grotesque apparitions that haunted their dreams, rendering them inconsolable and incapable of their daily tasks.

Desperation led the Hildebrand family to attempt an exorcism. They performed a ritual designed to expel the evil spirits from the girls' bodies, trapping them in a sack. The sack would then be cut into pieces with a sharp axe, theoretically banishing the witchcraft. But their efforts were in vain, and the malevolent influence persisted.

In their desperation, the Hildebrand sisters accused their neighbor, Nancy Evans, of being a witch. Panic began to spread through the community. If Nancy Evans were indeed a witch, she could cast spells on anyone. The townsfolk demanded justice from the local magistrate.

Ohio had no specific laws concerning witches or witchcraft at the time, so the justice had to devise a unique trial. He commissioned the construction of a large, crude scale and gathered the Hildebrands and concerned townspeople around it. In one hand, he held a Bible, and in the other, he had Nancy Evans take her place on the scale.

The justice declared, "So I will place this Holy Bible on one side of this scale, and seat Miss Evans on the other. If the Bible is heavier, we will know to drive her from our midst forever." The crowd roared in agreement.

As anticipated, Nancy Evans outweighed the Bible, and the fears of the townsfolk were temporarily quelled. It was a clever way for the justice to restore peace without resorting to violence or witch hunts.

After the Bethel trial, Nancy Evans and her family departed for Brown County, while the Hildebrands also vanished from the historical record.

Old Man Stout

In Tennessee's 228-year history, only one witch trial has been documented, unfolding in 1835 in Jamestown, in Fentress County. The central figure in this peculiar tale was an elderly recluse named Joseph Stout, who spent his days engrossed in philosophical and religious books within the walls of his cabin by the Obed River.

Dubbed "Old Man Stout," he became the subject of local curiosity as children would surreptitiously observe him reading by candlelight, an activity perceived as mysterious since he wasn't part of the local church. Rumors spread that this introverted man possessed supernatural abilities, capable of transforming into smoke and slipping through keyholes.

The turning point came when Rebecca French, a girl from a prominent family in the area fell mysteriously ill. Old Man Stout was asked if he could help the girl so he went to pay the family a visit. Strangely, when he arrived, Rebecca began to tremble. At that point her father demanded that Stout turn over his belt. Begrudgingly, Stout handed it over. When it was placed around Rebecca, she began to feel better. Rebecca's father then demanded that Stout take his daughter by the hand and cure her, but Stout insisted that he didn't have the ability and left. Furious, Rebecca's father sought a warrant from Squire Joshua Owens on the accounts that . The magistrate, swayed by the notion of witchcraft, issued an arrest warrant.

Under the cover of night, a posse armed with silver-cast bullets stormed Old Man Stout's cabin, resulting in a struggle that forced the outnumbered old man to the courthouse. There, battered and bruised, he pleaded not guilty to bewitching the girl. Witnesses testified to his alleged sorcery, recounting instances of spells cast on people and livestock. Squire Owens, deeming the evidence sufficient, forwarded the case to the circuit court.

In front of Judge Abraham Caruthers, Attorney General John B. McCormick surprisingly refused to prosecute Stout. Citing outdated statutes, the witch-hunters were rebuffed by Judge Caruthers, who clarified that such laws held no weight in Tennessee. Discontent ensued, with some speculating that Old Man Stout had enchanted the judge and attorney general.

Word spread throughout Jamestown, sparking rumors of Stout's mystical influence. Despite the near-riot in the courtroom, the accused witch returned to press charges against his assailants. In an unexpected turn, the jury, seemingly still under his 'spell,' ruled in favor of Stout, awarding him a significant sum.

Following this courtroom triumph, Old Man Stout withdrew from public view, occasionally reappearing to conduct business. Each time, witnesses claimed he vanished into a mysterious cloud of smoke, perpetuating the enigma surrounding this lone witch trial in Tennessee's history.

Legends

The Witch of the Carrabasett

In the 1700s in the wilderness of Northwest Maine, where the land held secrets that echoed with the ancient tales of Native Americans and early settlers, whispers told of the legend of the Witch of the Carrabasett. The mystical figure had the ability to shapeshift, seamlessly transitioning from a young maiden to a white timber wolf, and back again with an otherworldly grace.

This mysterious Native American witch, with piercing crystal blue eyes, was said to be accompanied by two guardian spirits. One, a "mikumwess" or dwarf, and the other, a ravenous bird whose eyes could discern travelers from miles away. Together, this formidable trio would transform into wolves, prowling the paths settlers traversed, leaving behind nothing but bones as a grim testament to their presence.

However, the Witch of the Carrabasett was not the sole enchantress in these mystical woods. Another figure, known as the Giant Witch, stood at a formidable seven feet tall, wielding powers greater than her shapeshifting counterpart. This towering witch lived in the surrounding mountains and, one day, decided to confront the Witch of the Carrabasett about her bloodthirsty actions.

The Giant Witch, driven by a sense of justice, approached the Witch of the Carrabasett, imploring her to cease the slaughter of Natives and find harmony with the inhabitants of the land. Yet, the plea fell on deaf ears, and the evil witch continued her ruthless ways.

One day, as a group of Native Americans hunted near the Seven Mile Stream, the Witch of the Carrabasett summoned her spirits. The trio transformed into wolves, swiftly killing the unsuspecting hunting party. The savagery of this act drew the ire of the Giant Witch. She arrived at the gruesome scene, resurrecting the fallen men and banishing the Witch of the Carrabasett to the east side of the stream as punishment.

Exiled from her homeland, the Witch of the Carrabasett underwent a transformation of her own. Altered by the consequences of her actions, she changed her ways. With the advent of the railroad in the area, a new chapter unfolded. Railroad workers, teetering on the brink of death, spoke of encounters with an elderly Native American woman with crystal clear blue eyes. Emerging mysteriously, she offered a potion from a blue pitcher. Miraculously, those who partook in this elixir found themselves revived and healed.

Legend has it that, to this day, the Giant Witch roams the west side of the stream, keeping vigilant watch to ensure the Witch of the Carrabasett remains reformed.

Whispers persist that the witch, yearning for redemption, seeks to mend ties with the Giant Witch, longing to return to her ancestral homeland and rewrite the narrative of her blood-stained past.

Marie Laveau

Marie Laveau, the legendary voodoo queen of New Orleans, was a woman whose life intertwined with the mystical and the practical, creating an enduring legacy that still captivates the city to this day.

Born on September 10, 1794, as the illegitimate daughter of Charles Laveau, a wealthy mulatto Creole plantation owner, and Marguerite D'Arcantel, a woman of African American and Choctaw Indian descent, Marie Laveau's early life was marked by her immersion in the world of herbs and their medicinal properties, a knowledge passed down by her grandmother.

In 1819, Marie married Jacques Paris, a free person of color from Haiti. They established their home in the French Quarter, and despite having two children, the marriage took a tragic turn when Paris mysteriously disappeared after five years. As a single mother, Laveau turned to work as a hairdresser and nurse's aide to support her family.

Marie Laveau's reputation as the voodoo queen began to blossom as she held spiritual ceremonies in Congo Square every Sunday. With a large snake named Zombi, she would dance, captivating the oppressed Black community of New Orleans. Rooted in African spirituality, Laveau's influence extended beyond spiritual gatherings to become a guiding force for people seeking advice on various matters.

Her home on St. Ann Street, as well as Congo Square, and the shores of Lake Pontchartrain were the primary sites for her rituals. At these locations, she provided counsel, conducted ceremonies, and invoked the spirit of the Great Zombi. Laveau's spiritual prowess was complemented by her role as a hairdresser, allowing her to glean information about the city's gossip and offer solutions to problems through her unique blend of voodoo and Catholic practices.

In a common-law marriage with Louis Christophe Dumesnil de Glapion, Laveau expanded her family to fifteen children. Despite her familial obligations, she became a prominent figure in the voodoo community, establishing Laveau's Voodoo Shop on Bourbon and St. Anne Marie. During the yellow fever outbreak, she used her knowledge of herbs to aid the afflicted.

Marie Laveau's earthly journey came to an end on June 15, 1881, within the walls of her home on Saint Ann Street. At the ripe age of 86, she departed this world, leaving behind a legacy that would echo through the ages. Her mortal remains found their resting place at plot 347 in the Glapion Family Crypt within St. Louis Cemetery #1.

Within the crypt, where over 80 souls rest, only 25 are related, while the others are comprised of friends and acquaintances of Laveau. These individuals, unable to afford a proper burial, found solace in the proximity to the voodoo queen's eternal presence.

Legend holds that Marie Laveau's spirit maintains a vigilant watch over her grave. Those who dare to disrespect her resting place are said to experience a spectral slap, a testament to the enduring power of the voodoo queen. A scattering of small rocks mysteriously thrown by unseen forces further contribute to the mystique surrounding the tomb.

Yet, for the majority who pilgrimage to Marie Laveau's final resting place, respect prevails. Many seekers, burdened by life's challenges, arrive in hopes of invoking her aid. Local lore prescribes a ritual for those in need: locate a stone or brick at her gravesite, mark the tomb with a red X, knock three times, and speak your desires. It is believed that, in time, these wishes will come true.

Alternative variations of the ritual involve drawing three Xs on the tomb, spinning thrice, knocking while vocalizing one's wish, or making a wish after drawing an X, covering it with one's hand, rubbing the foot against the tomb three times, tossing silver coins into a cup, and awaiting the desired outcome.

Visitors have left tokens of gratitude, ranging from bottles of alcohol, food, trinkets, charms, to even positive pregnancy tests. Monetary offerings, coins, and bills have also been left in appreciation of Laveau's spiritual influence. However, over the years, some have displayed less reverence. Incidents include attempts to glimpse Laveau's remains by dislodging bricks, and in December 2013, an audacious act of painting her tomb pink. Subsequent restoration efforts revealed a fascinating array of artifacts within the crypt, from human teeth and hair to money, lipstick, and even a bullet embedded in its aged walls.

Today, marking the tomb is discouraged to preserve its antiquity and prevent deterioration. Security measures, including the installation of cameras, were implemented due to the persistent marking of Xs by Laveau's followers. To view the tomb now requires a private tour with a registered guide.

Cato the Witch

Just outside of Carmi, Illinois, nestled along the banks of the Little Wabash River, stood a small, weather-worn wooden cabin. This small structure was home to an elderly woman known by the locals as Cato the Witch. Cato had lived a life full of hardship and solitude, raising several children who, upon reaching adulthood, distanced themselves from their eccentric mother, abandoning her in her twilight years.

Cato was both feared and revered in the area. Known for her knowledge of herbal remedies, she concocted various potions and mixtures to aid the sick and afflicted. Her remedies, derived from the wild herbs she foraged, brought relief to many, but they also earned her a reputation as a witch. The whispers of witchcraft grew louder with each passing year, fueled by her claims of conversing with spirits and seeing the ghosts of Native

Americans who once roamed the riverbanks. According to Cato, these spirits visited the ancient Indian mounds nearby, and at night, her ancestors and deceased relatives would come to her cabin, keeping a silent watch over her.

As Cato aged, her connection to the spectral world began to fade. Her once vivid encounters with ghosts became mere memories, and her health started to decline. Realizing her end was near, she journeyed to a nearby village to make her final arrangements. She expressed her desire for a unique burial: she wished to be placed in a coffin with a lid that was not screwed down that was to be buried only three feet deep. Her intent was clear — she wanted to come back to haunt her children since they abandoned her.

Not long after, Cato passed away. True to her wishes, she was buried in a grave near her cabin, close to the river she had known all her life. However, her death did not bring an end to the stories that surrounded her. The cabin did not fall silent; strange noises were often heard emanating from inside, and some villagers claimed to see Cato's figure moving through the windows, a ghostly presence bound to the place she had called home.

Her children, upon learning of her final wishes, never returned to visit her grave, fearing the promised haunting. Over the years, an unusual phenomenon was observed: catnip and wormwood, some of the very herbs Cato had used in her healing practices, began to grow abundantly on her grave.

Today, the exact location of Cato's cabin and grave has been lost to time, overgrown and forgotten. Yet, the story of Cato the Witch lingers in the local folklore.

The Witch of Meade County

In the quiet and mysterious corners of Meade County, Kentucky, in 1818, a baby girl named Leah Smock came into the world. She was born to a woman of alleged mysterious power, a witch who held considerable sway over the arcane. The identity of Leah's father remained elusive; save for the knowledge that he was a skilled cooper who crafted barrels destined to transport lime all the way to the far-off lands of Louisiana.

From a tender age, Leah exhibited a peculiar disposition, making her an odd, solitary child with few friends. Much of her early years were spent aiding her father in his barrel-making shop, until tragedy struck. Her father's life was cut short unexpectedly, leaving Leah to navigate the world as an orphaned child.

With no family but her enigmatic mother, Leah turned to the sprawling fields that surrounded their home, searching for wild berries and fruit to fill her days. Her connection with nature was palpable, and it would come to define her existence in more ways than one.

As her story unfolded, the people of Meade County would come to know Leah for her eccentricities and the aura of magic that surrounded her. Local children, ever curious, once ventured to her house and inadvertently stirred her ire. A careless act of picking up a seemingly insignificant stick in the corner of her home unleashed her fury. It was the "condon stick," a magical artifact that she and her mother used to weave spells and incantations.

Another incident involved Leah's visit to a neighbor's house. The moment she crossed the threshold, the neighbor's black cat was seized by an inexplicable frenzy. It hissed, spat, and clawed the moment it laid eyes on the girl. Leah's subsequent piercing shrieks filled the air as she chased the frantic feline until it disappeared forever, fleeing out the door.

Leah's reputation for mysticism and eccentricity grew with each passing year. She was said to possess the unnerving ability to predict death, and in some cases, cause it. It was a gift she displayed even in her childhood. One fateful day, she approached a farm and extended her hand to pet a horse. The owner, well aware of the tales that circulated about Leah and her mother, adamantly forbade her from making contact with the animal. Tragically, the very next day, the horse died suddenly. Whispers of a curse fell upon Leah, casting her in a sinister light.

Similar stories abounded, like the time she sought to hold a newborn baby boy after a neighbor had given birth. The infant's owner hesitated, sensing something ominous in Leah's presence. Sadly, their fear would be realized, as the child perished within a few days. Accusations of curses and malevolent powers began to plague Leah, further isolating her from the community.

Leah's actions extended beyond individuals to the very earth itself. Farmers spoke of her wrath when offended, telling tales of cursed lands, scorched by heatwaves and ravaged by droughts, all attributed to the mysterious powers she wielded.

Yet, it wasn't just curses and malevolence that Leah was known for. She had a rare gift, perhaps bestowed upon her by nature or some supernatural force. She was a healer, known for her potent herbal remedies and purportedly mystical abilities. While many shunned her, those in nearby villages quietly sought her out when they became ill.

The final chapter of Leah Smock's story unfolded on August 21, 1840, under peculiar circumstances. It was whispered throughout the community that her house had caught fire, and Leah had perished in the inferno. Some believed that villagers, weary of her perceived malevolence, had taken matters into their own hands, setting her cabin ablaze while she slept. Another dark account suggested she had been dragged into a smokehouse and burned alive.

Leah met her tragic end at the tender age of 22, and her earthly remains found their resting place in a small burial ground, perched atop a hill in Meade County. Her grave, however, bore a distinctive mark—a pointed headstone, an unmistakable sign labeling her as a witch.

Yet, even in death, Leah's story refused to fade into oblivion. A mere day after her burial, a local hunter claimed to have seen her spirit hovering over her grave, dressed in a white gown. As time passed, more and more residents of the county reported sightings of her ethereal presence. Fearful that her restless spirit might wander beyond her grave, the townsfolk took precautions. They covered her burial site with a formidable two-foot-high pile of rocks, a makeshift prison to keep her spirit at bay.

Curiously, as the years slipped by, odd occurrences continued to haunt Leah's legacy. Barrels, reminiscent of those crafted by her father, were discovered scattered in the woods near her grave. Equally baffling, the rocks that were intended to anchor her spirit gradually disappeared, one by one, as if Leah herself were moving them one by one from her final resting place.

Decades passed, and Leah's legend persisted. In the mid-20th century, Shirley Bennett, a longtime resident of Battletown, recalled his encounter with the Leah. He described the witch as having long black hair and a flowing white robe with black ties around her throat and waist. However, other locals who claimed to have seen her could barely discern her features; she appeared as a blurry, indistinct figure.

To this day, the people of Meade County speak of Leah Smock with a mix of reverence and trepidation. Hunters still claim to catch glimpses of her elusive spirit amidst the dense woods, and the barrels and rocks remain enigmatic reminders of a life that straddled the boundaries between reality and the supernatural.

The Bell Witch

The Bell Witch legend is a famous American folklore tale that originated in Adams, Tennessee, during the early 19th century. The story revolves around the Bell family, primarily John Bell and his daughter Betsy Bell, who claimed to be tormented by a malevolent spirit known as the Bell Witch.

John Bell, a man of influence in the local community, not only managed a prosperous farm but also served as a leader in the local church. He was involved in politics, holding a position as a justice of the peace and a farmer who was well-regarded in the Robertson County area.

In 1817 the Bell family started experiencing inexplicable and eerie occurrences that would later become the hallmark of the Bell Witch legend. Initially, the disturbances were dismissed as odd but inconsequential events — strange noises like knocking on doors, the sound of chains being dragged through the house, and even the unsettling noise of rats gnawing on bedposts.

Around this same time, John Bell reported encountering a strange creature in the woods near his home in 1817. Descriptions vary, but it's often portrayed as a creature with the body of a dog and the head of a rabbit. This bizarre encounter added another layer to the growing sense of unease and fear within the Bell family.

As time passed, however, the disturbances intensified, and the Bells claimed to have come into contact with a malevolent entity that identified itself as the "Bell Witch." This entity, often described as having a sinister, female voice, began communicating with the family, displaying an intimate knowledge of their private conversations and the ability to mimic voices.

The Bell Witch's focus seemed to center on John Bell, and the entity's actions took a toll on his health. He suffered from unexplained twitching and jerking, and his overall well-being rapidly declined. The entity openly declared its intent to kill John Bell, claiming responsibility for his deteriorating health.

John Bell

Amidst these disturbances, Betsy Bell, one of John and Lucy Bell's daughters, found herself at the center of speculation. Rumors circulated about a possible romance between Betsy and a neighbor named Joshua Gardner. The Bell Witch, displaying a penchant for meddling in the family's affairs, reportedly disapproved of this relationship. Some accounts suggest that the entity tormented Betsy, creating additional tension in her budding romance with Joshua Gardner.

News of the strange happenings spread, attracting visitors and skeptics alike. Many reported witnessing bizarre phenomena, such as objects moving on their own and unexplained noises, further fueling the mystery surrounding the Bell Witch. The entity's interactions with visitors were often aggressive, displaying a particular disdain for certain individuals.

In 1820, John Bell succumbed to the mysterious affliction that had plagued him. The Bell Witch took credit for his death, stating that it had poisoned him. After John Bell's death, the disturbances ceased, but the entity left with a chilling promise — it would return in seven years. True to its word, the disturbances resumed in 1828 but eventually faded away.

The Bell Witch legend has left an enduring mark on American folklore, inspiring numerous books, articles, and adaptations. The story has been explored in various mediums, from movies to plays, and continues to captivate the imagination.

Andrew Jackson Comes to Adams

After triumphing over the British in New Orleans during the War of 1812, Andrew Jackson sought a new adventure upon his return to middle Tennessee. Whispers of the Bell Witch in Adams, Tennessee, had captivated the region, and undeterred by fear, "Old Hickory" decided to investigate the veracity of these eerie tales.

General Andrew Jackson

Embarking on an overnight journey with companions, they traversed the moonlit roads through Springfield, eventually arriving at the mysterious locale of Adams.

Yet, when they approached within a hundred yards of Bell's home, an unexplained force halted Jackson's horse and carriage. Perplexed, the wheels seemed mechanically sound and the horse quite healthy, but an unseen resistance held them in place. The driver did his best to urge the horses along, but they wouldn't budge an inch.

Exiting the carriage to inspect the situation, Jackson and his comrades began to push the wagon with all their might. Yet as they shoved as hard as they could, Jackson stopped and began inspecting the wagon and wheels himself. At that point the men were met with an otherworldly voice declaring, "You can go now, General." Miraculously, the horses resumed their journey. Bewildered and spooked, Jackson curtailed his visit. As dawn broke the next day, Jackson and his entourage swiftly departed Adams, heading back to the familiar grounds of his mansion, the Hermitage.

Mother Fisher

In the mid-19th century, deep in the heart of Lancaster County, Pennsylvania, nestled in the mountains away from civilization, lived a woman shrouded in mystery and whispers of the supernatural—Barbara Fisher, known by the locals as "Mother Fisher." Wrinkled, hunched, with a cascade of white hair and a few long strands protruding from her chin, Mother Fisher was said to be disagreeable and vindictive, possessing mystical powers granted, as the local lore claimed, in exchange for mortgaging her soul to the devil.

Mother Fisher's solitary existence was accompanied by a 300-year-old book, a family heirloom from Germany, filled with spells and arcane knowledge. Her reputation for helping those with sick children added a layer of complexity to her enigmatic persona. She would heal the ailing youngsters, displaying a softness rarely seen, but her dealings with adults were marked by disdain, with assistance only granted for a fee.

For those who sought her services in recovering stolen horses, Mother Fisher offered a peculiar divination method. Taking three hairs from the tail of the pilfered horse, she would set them ablaze on a shovel. The direction of the burning hairs allegedly pointed to the thief's whereabouts. While she claimed to cast spells to ensure the return of the stolen animals, success was rare. Failed attempts were blamed on the supposed lack of faith of the horse owner.

Potions to induce love, spells to curse enemies, and the ability to make normal, healthy cows produce bloody milk were among Mother Fisher's infamous offerings, all requiring a nominal fee. Legend had it that crossing her or eliciting her anger could lead to calamities such as droughts or the sudden demise of entire herds of farm animals.

The saga took an unexpected turn when a prominent farmer, embroiled in disputes with Mother Fisher, sued her after his dog perished under mysterious circumstances. He alleged that Mother Fisher cursed the dog and demanded a substantial sum to lift the curse. The judge, surprisingly, allowed the lawsuit to proceed.

A local witness, warned by Mother Fisher not to testify, defied her warning and faced dire consequences. His well ran dry, his cows produced bloody milk, and his infant fell gravely ill.

When summoned to defend herself, Mother Fisher, rather than denying the accusations, proclaimed her guilt. The judge sided with the farmer, awarding him $3 plus court costs.

Mother Fisher's enigmatic existence came to an end in early November 1888, as she passed away at the age of 89.

Sadie Baker

In the mid-19th century, Manchester, Tennessee witnessed a mysterious arrival that would shroud the village in a cloak of tragedy and folklore.

It began with the appearance of a mute woman who wore tattered clothing. Starvation etched her features, and desperation guided her to beg for coins on the streets.

One prominent family, their hearts touched by compassion, decided to extend a hand to the destitute young woman. Taking her into their home, they washed away the grime of the streets, clothed her in dignity, and fed her until her hunger was but a distant memory. In the glow of newfound care, the woman transformed into a vision of elegance, her astonishing beauty a stark contrast to her initial ragged appearance.

However, this tale of charity and redemption took a dark turn. Olivia, the eldest daughter, was entwined in a courtship with a young man of wealth. Yet, the mere sight of the reformed woman ignited a passion in him, leading to a heart-wrenching decision to break up with Olivia.

As Olivia's heart shattered, her mother, desperate to mend her daughter's wounds kicked the mute woman out of their home and convinced a local preacher that she was a witch. This insidious notion took root, leading to a sinister plan to rid the village of the alleged enchantress.

One fateful day, a somber procession, composed of misguided congregation members and the very family that had once shown compassion, forcibly escorted the mute woman to Concord Cemetery. A hastily dug grave awaited her, and without remorse, they cast her into the abyss, burying her alive beneath a cascade of freshly turned soil. In her final act of defiance, the mysterious woman locked eyes with Olivia and shouted, "I am Sadie Baker!"

A weighty stone sealed her tomb, ensuring her supposed witchery could not escape.

The incident left an indelible mark on Manchester, but life, as it often does, pressed on. Days melted into months, and months into years. Olivia eventually reconciled with her wealthy suitor and found marital bliss. However, the echoes of that traumatic day lingered. Sadie Baker, once entombed in soil, seemed to transcend the grave, haunting Olivia's every reflection and dwelling.

As time unfolded, Olivia's sanity unraveled, thread by thread, until the fabric of her mind could no longer withstand the spectral presence of Sadie. A darkness descended upon her soul, necessitating her confinement in a local asylum.

To this day, Sadie Baker's resting place remains in Concord Cemetery in Tullahoma. A modest headstone stands as a testament to a life wrongly condemned, and a large rock, placed by those who remember the tale, guards her eternal rest.

Locals speak of a haunting ritual, where placing a coin on Sadie's grave and whispering "I am Sadie Baker" three times will cause her spirit to appear in the humble burying ground.

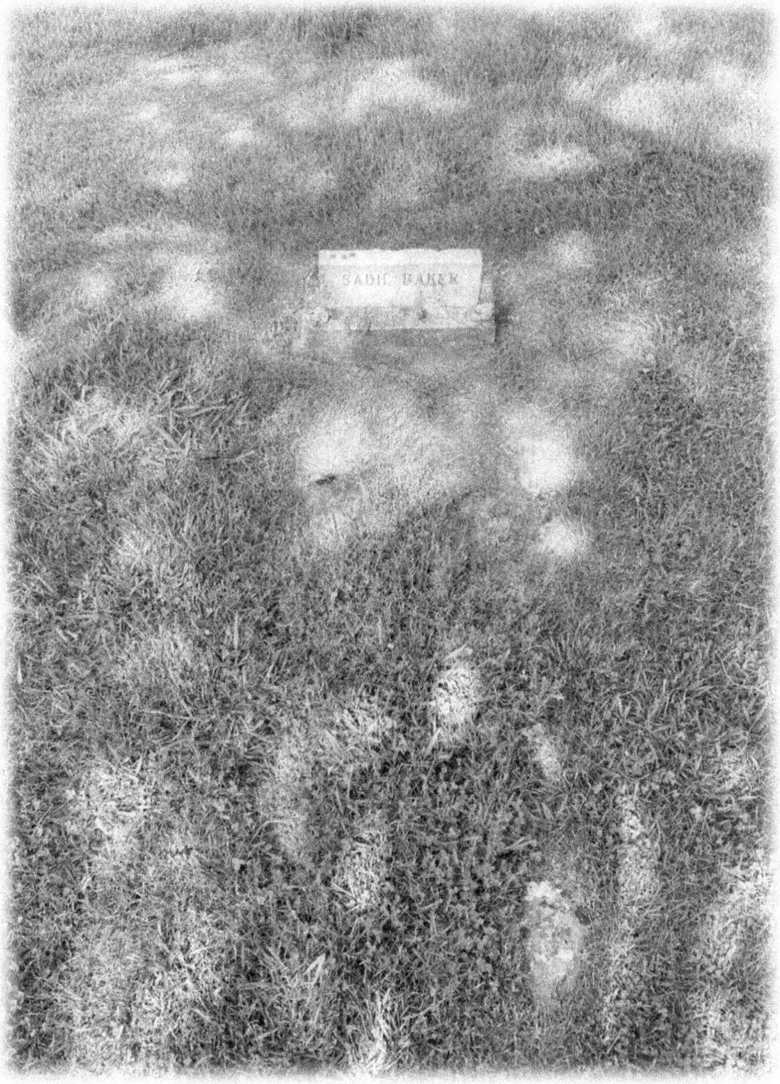

The Witches Tree

In the heart of Old Louisville, Kentucky at the intersection of Sixth Street and Park Avenue, stands the enigmatic Witches Tree, a testament to a bygone era when gypsies once converged upon the city. Though the twisted tree itself is a relatively recent addition, its roots delve into the late 19th century, weaving a tale of ancient practices, warnings unheeded, and the enduring legacy of mystical retribution.

Legend has it that a group of gypsies, who were also practitioners of Wicca, made an annual pilgrimage to Louisville every spring. Their chosen meeting spot was a tall maple tree where they would gather to socialize, conjure spells, and celebrate the arrival of May Day.

The year was 1889, and city officials, in a nod to tradition, decided to erect a pole in honor of May Day. Unfortunately, the chosen location for this pole happened to be the site of the beloved maple tree.

City leaders, oblivious to the cultural significance of the tree to the gypsies, decided to cut it down. The gypsies, enraged by the disrespect shown to their sacred space, attempted to voice their concerns to the mayor and other officials. However, societal biases prevailed, and the gypsies, deemed of a lesser class, were not granted a face-to-face meeting.

Undeterred, the gypsies solemnly vowed that if their cherished tree fell, calamity would follow. Sadly, the warning went unheeded, and the maple tree was chopped down. The immediate aftermath saw no apparent repercussions, and life in Louisville continued unaffected by the gypsies' threats.

Yet, when the gypsies returned the following spring, they enacted their vengeance. Chanting in unison, the women cast a powerful spell that summoned a massive storm, unleashing several tornadoes upon the city.

The storm, which struck on May 27, 1890, wreaked havoc, destroying numerous homes and buildings and claiming several lives.

Tornado Damage 1890
Courtesy of Library of Congress

In the center of Old Louisville, where the maple tree once stood, a sudden burst of lightning hit the old tree stump.

In the days that followed, a peculiar sapling emerged, distinct from its predecessor. Unlike the once-beautiful maple, this new tree was twisted and gnarled.

Today, the Witches Tree has become a focal point of local lore, attracting visitors who leave behind beads, statues, trinkets, and offerings in its bark and branches. This act is believed to bring good luck, with some seeking healing or placing items of departed loved ones to aid in the grieving process. The tree, though lacking a ghostly tale, is said to carry a curse. Those who dare to pilfer trinkets or offerings risk inviting terrible misfortune into their lives.

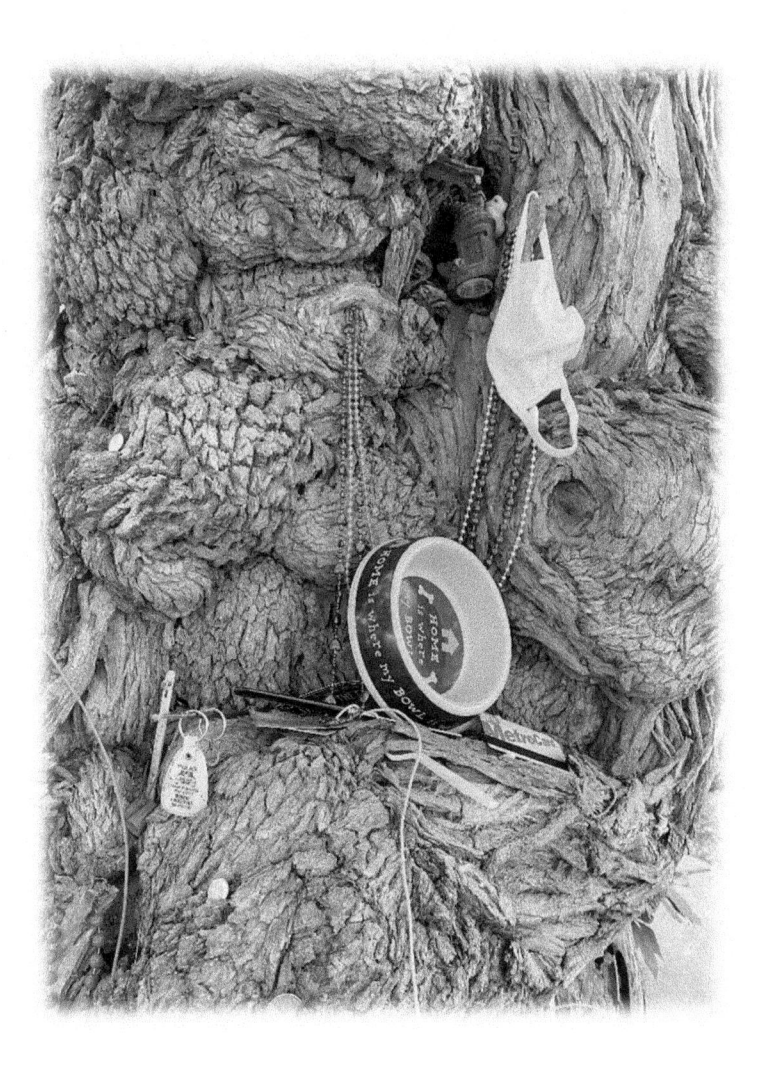

Yet, the phenomenon doesn't end with the Witches Tree alone. A nearby bush has become an unintended receptacle for additional offerings, a place where you can find the overflow from the enchanted tree.

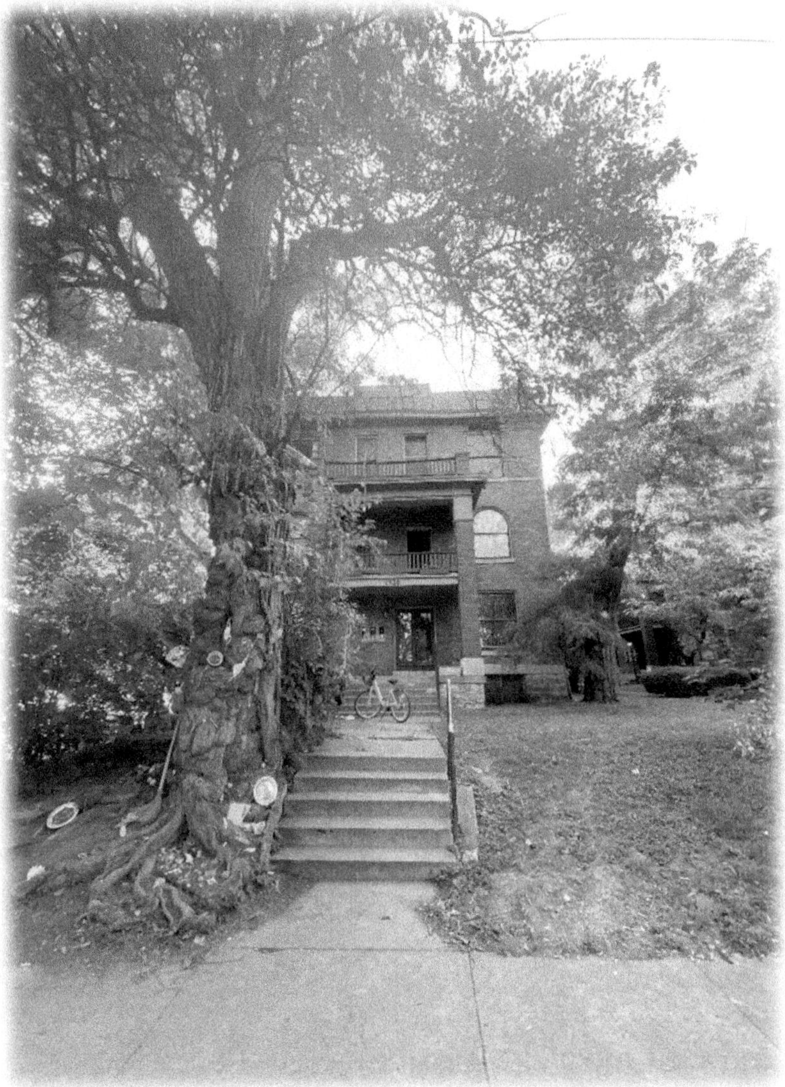

Curses & Spells

The River of Death

The story of the curse of the Saco River is woven into the rich tapestry of its long history, dating back nearly 10,000 years. Evidence of human habitation in the Saco River valley can be traced to ancient times, with documented settlement by Native Americans, particularly the Pigwacket kin-based group, dating back to 1642.

The valley, cradled in the embrace of northeastern New Hampshire and southwestern Maine, witnessed the passage of major Native American trails.

The Saco River
Photo Courtesy of Library of Congress

The Saco River itself, coursing through a rural expanse of 1,703 square miles of forests and farmlands, meanders west and southwest of Portland before gracefully emptying into the Atlantic Ocean at Saco Bay, a journey spanning 136 miles from its source.

The river's history is intertwined with Squando, the sagamore of the Sokokis, a figure perceived as both seer and magician by the indigenous people. Despite counseling a peaceful approach towards the white settlers, Squando harbored a deep-seated resentment following a great wrong done to him.

Legend intertwines with history as the tale unfolds. Squando's wife and infant son, heirs to the chiefdom of the Saco tribe, were traveling by canoe near the river's mouth. A fateful encounter with three rowdy, drunken English sailors marked a turning point. The sailors, in a disturbing wager, questioned whether Native American babies could swim at birth. In a horrifying act, one of the men snatched the infant and threw him into the river to test this belief.

The mother, in desperate pursuit, dove into the water to rescue her child. After an agonizing interval, she emerged with the baby, but the child succumbed to the trauma a few days later. In his grief, Squando, a man of great spiritual influence, walked to the riverbanks.

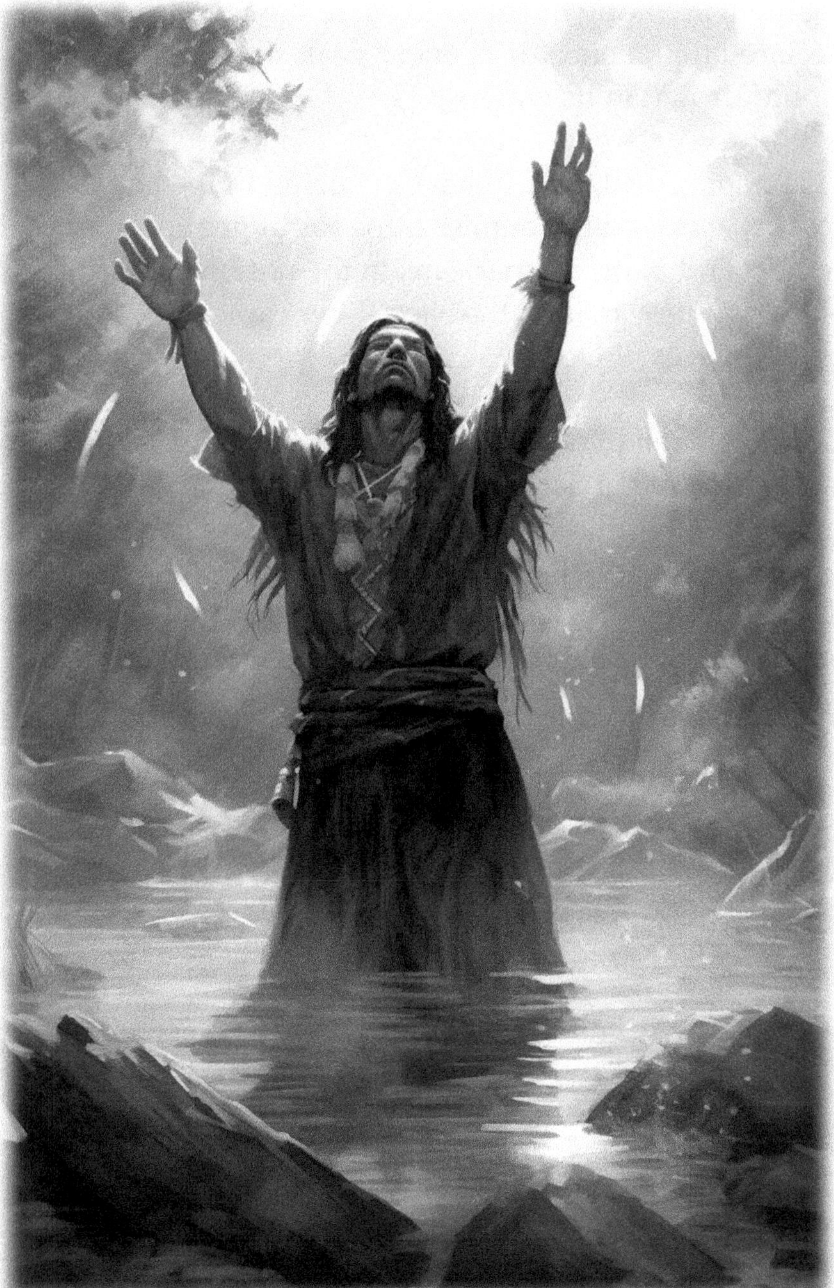

Sobbing and lifting his hands high in the air, Squando chanted, invoking the gods to curse the Saco River. He declared that, henceforth, every year, three white people would drown in its waters.

This tragic event, said to have occurred in the late 17th century, marked the demise of peaceful relations between settlers and Native Americans in the region. According to Native American lore, the Saco River came to be known as "The River of Death."

Despite its relatively shallow waters, the curse endured. Year after year, a handful of people succumb to the river's treacherous currents, as if Squando's lament continues to echo through time, reminding those who dare to traverse its waters of the tragedy that befell his family and the lasting legacy of sorrow that blankets the Saco River.

Buck's Grave

In the early years of Bucksport, Maine, the town's founding figure, Colonel Jonathan Buck, stood as a pillar of influence and community leadership. Born on February 20, 1719, in Woburn, Massachusetts, Colonel Buck's life unfolded as a tapestry of devotion to his Puritan beliefs, familial commitment as a loving husband and father of nine, and impactful contributions to the economic growth of the region.

Colonel Buck's endeavors extended to the establishment of essential infrastructure, including a sawmill, a grist mill, and a general store, marking him as a Revolutionary War hero and earning him the esteemed position of Justice of the Peace. Despite these commendable achievements, his legacy became entwined with a tale of darkness that would tarnish his name for the rest of eternity.

In the annals of local lore, a chilling story emerged — a narrative of accusation, witchcraft, and a curse that would transcend time. The tale spoke of a woman, linked in various accounts to Colonel Buck by threads of romance or forbidden connection. Accused of practicing sorcery, she was sentenced to death by a jury of her peers which included Buck.

As the hangman paced back and forth waiting to cut the rope that would hurl the condemned woman into eternity, the defiant convicted witch turned her gaze towards Colonel Buck. In a moment of anguish and revenge, she cast upon him a curse that reverberated through the ages. "Johnathan Buck, you will soon die and over your grave they will erect a stone. Upon that stone, the imprint of my foot shall appear," she declared, "and for all time after your accursed race has vanished from the face of the earth, will the people from far and near know that you murdered a woman!"

The haunting prophecy took tangible form on the Blue Hill granite monument erected in Colonel Buck's memory in 1852. A month after its placement, a spectral leg and foot-shaped stain materialized — a ghostly testament to the dark chapter that unfolded in the town's history.

City officials, attempting to expunge the eerie mark, found their efforts thwarted. Instead of fading, the imprint deepened over the years, becoming an enduring symbol of the spectral connection between Colonel Jonathan Buck and the woman he condemned.

The haunting stain, like an ethereal footprint on history, persisted, whispering of a time when the supernatural collided with the earthly, leaving an indelible mark on Bucksport.

Mother Nance

In the rugged and remote mountains of Macon County, North Carolina, during the late 1700s, the mysterious figure of Old Nance, a purported witch with Cherokee roots, cast a long shadow over the local folklore. Known to the mountain folk as Mother Nance, she resided in a weathered log cabin perched at the top of a mountain.

Legend has it that the tale of Old Nance took a twist when a young lady from the region fell deeply in love with a boy from South Carolina. However, the girl's mother vehemently opposed the match and was determined to prevent her daughter from eloping with the young man who hailed from a different state. In her quest to intervene, the mother dragged her daughter up the mountain to Mother Nance's secluded cabin, hoping to thwart the impending union.

Witches, as local beliefs held, harbored a deep disdain for marriages and would go to great lengths to obstruct them. As the girl and her mother stood in the presence of Mother Nance, she promptly ordered the mother to leave the cabin. Once alone with the girl, Mother Nance performed a peculiar ritual. She scraped a turnip and instructed the girl to eat it. Strangely, as soon as the first scraping touched the girl's tongue, an inexplicable pain gripped her nose. The discomfort quickly spread across her cheek, nearly reaching her ears. Alarmed, the mother was summoned back into the cabin, and the distorted girl returned home.

The peculiar events took an even stranger turn as the girl ventured out of the house. Passersby couldn't help but stare, for her once-normal nose was now hideously misshapen. The South Carolina beau paid her a visit one day. However, the young lady wore a cloak and hid her face with her hands. The gentleman caller playfully prodded and begged to see his true love's face.

Sadly, when she revealed herself, he was horrified at her altered appearance, and abandoned her in disgust.

Distraught, the mother returned to Mother Nance, pleading for a remedy. Unfazed, the mysterious witch administered more turnip scrapings to the girl, who willingly consumed them. Miraculously, her nose returned to its original form. However, Mother Nance issued a solemn warning: should the girl attempt to marry again, the ghastly disfigurement would return, and she would lose her lover.

In a rare trip to town to acquire herbs, Mother Nance encountered an unexpected adversary — a bull belonging to a local farmer named Carr McDordle. The bull, without warning, charged at Mother Nance.

Instead of succumbing to panic, she turned around and fixed the creature with a menacing glare. To everyone's astonishment, the bull halted in its tracks, overcome with fear, and hastily retreated.

That night, the bull, now disoriented and agitated, began recklessly ramming into trees and rocks. As darkness descended, the animal sprinted at full speed and collided with two trees, becoming hopelessly lodged between them. The local farmers, unable to extricate the bull, witnessed the strange power that seemed to emanate from Mother Nance. Once the bull finally died, the buzzards picked the bones (and the tree) clean.

Over time, the tales of Mother Nance circulated through hushed whispers, and fear of her mysterious powers kept the locals at bay.

The Witch of Roan Mountain

In the early 1800s, nestled on the border between Tennessee and North Carolina, Roan Mountain loomed high, shrouded in mystery and whispers of an old haggard woman known simply as "the witch." This mysterious figure, dubbed the Witch of Roan Mountain, was said to inhabit a cave on the mountain, casting a formidable shadow over the lives of those who called the mountain home.

For the locals, the Witch of Roan Mountain was a source of fear and trepidation. The mountain dwellers lived in perpetual dread of the witch, offering her unwavering submission. In a display of deep-seated fear, they gave her food and gifts in a desperate attempt to appease her supernatural powers. The mere utterance of her name was believed to trigger calamities—droughts, landslides, floods, or lightning strikes—often resulting in immediate misfortune or death for the unfortunate summoner.

One day, the mountain community decided to have a picnic. When the witch got wind of the event and decided to attend, chaos erupted. A riot ensued, and many attendees were injured and trampled as panic ensued, horses charging in all directions.

In the face of such superstitions, there was one man who dared to defy the fear. Old Man Crowse, residing a few miles from the witch's cave, openly expressed his skepticism under the influence of moonshine, claiming not to care about the witch's powers. Little did he know his casual dismissal would lead to his own bewitchment. The locals recounted that the old sorceress "witched him clean crazy," subjecting him to periods of speechlessness followed by manic episodes where he would run in all weather, until collapsing from exhaustion.

This spell persisted for a staggering seven years, a testament to the perceived power of the Witch of Roan Mountain.

The Witch of Roan Mountain met her demise at the hands of an unexpected adversary—modern technology.

In the lore of the mountain, it was believed that those bewitched by her could seek the services of a witch doctor to lift the curse. This mystical practitioner would draw her image on a paper, pin it to a tree, and shoot it with a silver bullet to break the spell.

In an unforeseen turn of events, a traveling photographer crossed paths with the witch and, against her wishes, captured her image. Unaware of the supernatural implications, the photograph found its way into the hands of the local witch doctor. Called upon to lift a spell, the witch doctor took the photograph, pinned it to a tree and shot it with a silver bullet. The incident had unintended consequences—people out picking berries discovered the lifeless body of the Witch of Roan Mountain lying near her cabin the following day.

The era of the mountain's mysterious sorceress had come to an end, marked by the clash of ancient folklore and the march of progress.

The Witch of Hedgehog Island

In the remote corners of southeast Maine, nestled near the Canadian border, a mysterious woman named Becky Murch lived on Hedgehog Island, earning her the ominous title of "The Witch of Hedgehog Island" in the 1830s. Becky, a recluse by choice, enjoyed her solitary existence surrounded by several cats and a multitude of chickens. Her home, crafted from driftwood and wood salvaged from sunken ships, stood as a testament to her resourcefulness.

Living off the land, Becky sustained herself through her garden, the fish she caught, and the clams she dug up along the lake's edge. Occasionally, she ventured to the mainland, to Jonesport, to trade for essentials. However, the people of Jonesport harbored an unkind opinion of Becky, considering her to be an embodiment of malevolence and witchcraft.

One day, Becky sought to trade with a prominent farmer in Jonesport, only to face rejection and scorn. The farmer, who had spurned her, found himself bedridden the next day, stricken with agonizing arthritis. A pervasive belief in the community emerged that Becky had cursed him. A constable, responding to the town's rumors, paid Becky a visit, warning her against causing further disturbances in Jonesport. Miraculously, the farmer's affliction lifted with the dawn, sparking an air of unease among the townsfolk.

Expelled from Jonesport, Becky's quest for trade led her to Androscoggin County, where her path intertwined with that of Horace Beals, a young farmer. Desiring to barter for a cow, Becky was lacking anything of value to offer in return and was asked to leave. Curiously, an hour after her departure, the very cow she sought fell to the ground, convulsing in an inexplicable bout of distress.

Hours later, as Horace attended to his ailing cow, Becky reappeared, offering to heal the sick cow. However, her request was steep – in exchange, Horace must surrender his fattest pig. Enraged by the audacity of the demand, Horace, driven by a surge of anger, brandished a whip and forcefully chased the old woman from his farm. Upon his return, the cruel irony unfolded as he discovered the lifeless form of his once-ailing cow. Strangely, that same afternoon, while feeding his pigs, Horace found that his once-plump sow had mysteriously died.

Confounded and desperate, Horace sought counsel from a local Native American reputed to be a witch doctor. In a grave revelation, the witch doctor speculated that the only means to stop Becky from cursing the farms in the area was her death. However, cognizant of the legal repercussions, the witch doctor refrained from advocating Horace to directly do any harm to Becky. Instead, he proposed an alternative solution and followed Horace home, prepared to thwart any potential threats should Becky return.

The following morning Becky returned to Horace's farm with a sinister ultimatum — surrender a sheep, or death would become an unwelcome constant on his property. Undeterred by the gravity of the threat, Horace, fueled by a surge of determination, seized his whip and forcefully expelled Becky from his farm once again. Becky retreated back home to Hedgehog Island, attending to her feline companions and feathery denizens.

True to the sinister premonition, Becky's departure ushered in a macabre twist of fate. Horace's largest sheep suddenly became very ill. The sudden sickness didn't kill the sheep instantly, it survived the night but as the morning came, it was struggling to breathe. Swiftly responding to the sheep's imminent death, the witch doctor hastily constructed a fiery altar. In a ritualistic spectacle, he meticulously dissected the dying sheep, extracting its heart, which he then suspended over the crackling flames.

Amidst this mystifying theater, Horace and a handful of bewildered neighbors bore witness to the witch doctor's pronouncement — Becky, it seemed, had shifted her malevolence into the hapless creature. The prescribed remedy for her ethereal entrenchment was the incineration of the sheep's heart, a symbolic act believed to induce the Witch of Hedgehog Island's demise, with her very heart consumed by internal flames.

In tandem with this occult spectacle, Becky, back on Hedgehog Island, succumbed to agonizing convulsions, desperately seeking comfort in a futile attempt to assuage the internal inferno. A concerned island neighbor, hearing her desperate cries, rushed to Becky's home. Bursting through the door, the neighbor encountered a harrowing scene, with Becky proclaiming, "I'm on fire from the inside!"

Summoned from the mainland, a doctor assessed Becky's frail state, attributing her condition to dehydration and malnutrition. Evacuated to the mainland for extensive treatment, Becky gradually recovered. Despite regaining her health, Becky never left Hedgehog Island again.

Meanwhile, Horace Beals, following the strange incident with the Witch of Hedgehog Island, sold his farm and pursued a career in the granite quarries of Rockland. As he worked diligently, he eventually secured the contract to build the United States Treasury Building in Washington, D.C., amassing a fortune.

Legend has it that on the day Horace signed the contract, Becky mysteriously disappeared from Hedgehog Island. Some speculate drowning, while others believe that the burning of the sheep's heart forged an unexplained link between Becky and Horace. As fate bestowed riches upon him, the Witch of Hedgehog Island vanished, a mysterious sacrifice to balance the scales of fortune.

The Hex Breakers

Blind Isom's Grim Diagnosis

In the early 1890s, a dark and mysterious chapter unfolded in Choctaw territory, which would later become part of Oklahoma. Stephen Belvin, the sheriff of Blue County, fell seriously ill with pneumonia. Unable to find help within his own village, he sought treatment in another town from a white doctor. The language barrier proved challenging, prompting Sheriff Belvin to hire Mary Folsom, a young woman of mixed Native and white heritage, to serve as his nurse. Mary diligently followed the doctor's orders, ensuring proper medication administration and around-the-clock care. Despite her efforts, Sheriff Belvin's condition showed no signs of improvement.

Desperation led the family to seek the counsel of Blind Isom, a renowned witch doctor. Blind Isom, after examining Sheriff Belvin, delivered a chilling verdict. He asserted that the white doctor was incapable of treating a Choctaw and claimed that a malevolent spell had been cast upon the sheriff. Shockingly, Blind Isom accused

Mary Folsom, the nurse, of being the witch behind the curse. He prophesied that as long as Mary cared for the sheriff, he would never recover. To break the spell and ensure his survival, Sheriff Belvin would have to take Mary's life with his own hands.

The weight of Blind Isom's words hung heavily in the air as the family grappled with a difficult decision. Faced with conflicting advice from the white doctor and the Choctaw witch doctor, Sheriff Belvin recognized the gravity of the situation. In a moment of inner turmoil, he pretended to be asleep while a relative handed him a knife. As Mary innocently checked on him during the night, Sheriff Belvin, torn between cultural beliefs and medical advice, carried out the grim act, hacking the young woman to death.

Strangely, Sheriff Belvin's health did improve, and he eventually made a full recovery. In the Choctaw territory, where he held the esteemed position of sheriff and was a respected leader, the murder of Mary Folsom went unpunished.

Oklahoma Vengeance

In the spring of 1899, near Grant, Oklahoma, a dark chapter unfolded in the community when an outbreak of spiral meningitis claimed the lives of several children, including the son of a highly esteemed local pastor, Solomon Hotema. Hotema, born in 1851 to a Choctaw family that had immigrated from Mississippi, had dedicated his life to the Presbyterian church. He studied at Roanoke College in Virginia before ultimately becoming an ordained preacher.

However, a flaw in Hotema's character would soon play a pivotal role in a series of horrific events. His unfortunate penchant for alcohol, which occasionally led to combative behavior, would set the stage for a disturbing chapter in the community's history.

As the town grappled with the devastating outbreak of spiral meningitis, a meeting convened at the church to seek guidance on halting the deaths. Sam Tarnatubby, a renowned witch doctor in the region, was consulted. Following discussions with village elders, Tarnatubby delivered a grim diagnosis: the children had fallen victim to a death spell cast by witches, and to break the curse, these alleged witches must be killed. The dilemma got even more complicated when the community leaders realized that some of their own relatives might be implicated as witches.

Solomon Hotema, swayed by Tarnatubby's ominous counsel as well as his inebriated state, enlisted two full-blooded Choctaw companions, Tobias Williams and Sam Frye, to join him in a mission to eliminate the purported witches. Armed with a rifle and shotgun, the trio embarked on a fateful journey in Hotema's buggy.

Their first target was Vina Coleman, Hotema's sister-in-law. In a tragic encounter, Vina was shot and killed while cradling her baby. The violence escalated as the men moved to Hall Greenwood's residence. Greenwood rushed outside to greet his friends, but the trio demanded that he turn his wife over to be executed. Despite Greenwood's pleas for mercy, his wife was mercilessly gunned down in front of him.

The bloodshed continued with a visit to the home of Alfred Morris, another reputed sorcerer, who was left for dead after a barrage of bullets. The men then sought out Eastman Mississippi, another alleged witch, but his absence spared him from the violent fate that befell the others.

Shortly after the murders, Solomon Hotema surrendered to the authorities, acknowledging responsibility for the deaths. He confessed to having murdered three individuals known as witches, believing they had caused the plague that was killing the children. Sam Tarnatubby, charged as an accessory, was implicated for advising the deadly mission. The trio, including Tobias Williams and Sam Frye, found themselves behind bars.

While awaiting trial, Tobias Williams succumbed to a mysterious ailment, likely a consequence of the unsanitary conditions in the cramped jail. In a surprising turn of events, the jury acquitted Sam Tarnatubby of being an accessory, attributing the defendants' actions to insanity during the homicides. Despite separate indictments for each victim, Hotema and Frye were acquitted of the murders of Greenwood and Morris.

The unexpected outcome shocked both the defense and prosecuting attorneys. Hotema, however, was found guilty of killing Vina Coleman and sentenced to death by hanging on February 14, 1902. However, Judge T.C. Humphrey of Hugo successfully appealed to President William McKinley, securing a commutation to life imprisonment.

Samuel Hotema breathed his last breath in 1907 and was interred in the Atlanta Federal Penitentiary Prison Cemetery in Georgia, leaving behind a haunting tale of tragedy, superstition, and the blurred lines between justice and vengeance.

The Ninth Day

In the fall of 1895, Trieble Laub, an elderly Dutch man residing in Bethlehem, Pennsylvania, fell gravely ill. Months of bedridden existence took a toll on him, and when strength returned to his frail body, Trieble decided to embark on a journey to Reading in search of a hexa doctor, a witch doctor believed to wield incredible power.

The hexa doctor, a mystical figure steeped in the dark arts, examined Trieble and delivered a disconcerting revelation. A potent curse, the result of malevolent intentions, had been cast upon him. However, the enigmatic hexa doctor assured Trieble that he had reversed the curse and placed it on the person who gave it to him. The elderly man, bewildered and insistent on living harmoniously in his town, adamantly declared that he had no known enemies.

Undeterred, the hexa doctor foretold that upon Trieble's return home, on the ninth day, the individual responsible for the curse would reveal themselves at his doorstep.

True to the prophecy, on that fateful morning, a resounding knock echoed through the air. Eager to confront his mysterious adversary, Trieble swung the door open to find his neighbor, George Winch, standing before him.

George, having visited Trieble to purchase wood for the impending winter, was met with unexpected hostility. Trieble, convinced that George was the source of his affliction, launched into a torrent of curses and threats against him. Confused and unsettled, George withdrew, returning to the sanctuary of his own home.

The following day, Lovine Laub, Trieble's son, approached the town physician with an ominous message. He informed the doctor that he would soon be treating George Winch, advising him to be prepared for an unannounced visit as George would be severely ill.

Perplexed by this cryptic warning, the doctor visited George, only to find him in good health.

However, when the doctor arrived at George's residence, he found no signs of the predicted ailment. George, in apparent good health, greeted the physician with genuine surprise. Perplexed, the doctor shared Lovine's ominous message about an alleged curse placed upon George. The revelation angered George; a man deeply connected to his spirituality.

Rather than confronting his neighbor directly, George chose to avoid the Lovines, steering clear of potential conflict. However, the quietude was short-lived. Within days, unsettling whispers permeated the town, revealing that Trieble Laub had openly branded George as a witch during a town picnic. This affront to George's character was intolerable, and he resolved to take decisive action to protect his reputation.

Incensed by the defamation, George Winch decided to take legal action against Trieble Laub. He enlisted the services of William H. Snowden, a former Pennsylvania congressman, and filed a lawsuit seeking $5,000 in damages for the harm inflicted upon his character.

The outcome of the legal proceedings remains shrouded in mystery, as no court records provide clarity on the resolution or whether a judge even entertained the case. Records suggest that George Winch, branded a witch, chose to leave the area the following year as he moved to a neighboring town.

The Pow-Wow Doctor

During the summer of 1928, Milton Hess, a farmer from York County, Pennsylvania found himself grappling with unsettling issues on his farm. His cows stopped producing milk and his chickens were no longer laying eggs. Seeking a solution, he turned to a local "pow-wow doctor" named John Blymyre. In a detailed account of his predicament, Hess explained the troubling events occurring on his land. Blymyre, presenting himself as a practitioner of magical arts, diagnosed the situation as a curse plaguing the farm. Blymyre consulted a local witch named Emma Knapp from Lancaster County. She gave him a vision that revealed another witch, a local farmer named Nelson Rehmeyer, who was causing Hess' problems.

Blymyre, backed by the endorsement of his teenage pupil, John Curry, assured Hess that for a fee of $40, he could lift the hex afflicting the farm. Convinced of Blymyre's supposed mystical abilities, Milton Hess initially provided $10 and promised to settle the remaining $30 later. Weeks later, Blymyre returned, asserting that he had performed a ritual that had successfully broken the curse. However, skepticism arose as Hess recounted that his troubles had intensified, including a recent incident where his chicken coop was robbed, and several chickens were stolen.

Undeterred, Blymyre offered an explanation, claiming that the source of the ongoing issues lay with Rehmeyer. Blymyre asserted that the only effective remedy was to obtain a lock of Rehmeyer's hair and bury it eight feet deep beneath the ground behind the Hess chicken coop.

Milton Hess, confronted with the urgency of resolving the curse on his farm, dispatched his 18-year-old son, Wilbert, along with Blymyre and John Curry, to procure a lock of hair from the alleged source of the hex, Nelson Rehmeyer.

On November 27, 1928, the trio forcefully entered Rehmeyer's residence in North Hopewell township, instigating a violent confrontation with the unsuspecting farmer.

Amid the ensuing chaos, the startled Rehmeyer, under the mistaken impression of a robbery, threw his wallet to the intruders. Strangely, they displayed no interest in the wallet's contents. To further intensify the bizarre scenario, John Curry, the youngest of the group, callously seized Rehmeyer's wallet and tossed it into the fireplace.

A few minutes later the trio left, but they didn't leave with a lock of his hair.

Two days later, concern for Rehmeyer's well-being prompted a neighbor, Oscar Glafelter, to visit his residence. To his grisly discovery, Glafelter found the charred remains of Rehmeyer sprawled in the kitchen, adding a macabre twist to the unfolding narrative.

The subsequent police investigation quickly zeroed in on John Blymyre, who had a reputation as someone who dabbled in the dark arts. Blymyre, however, proved to be more than just a practitioner of folk magic; he was, in reality, mentally unstable, harboring delusions of being a witch with supernatural powers. Upon digging into his history, authorities learned that Blymyre had spent a six-week stint in a mental hospital in 1923, followed by a successful escape attempt. York County laws dictated that after a year post-escape, the individual was absolved of any charges and not liable to be returned to the asylum.

John Blymyer

The investigation also unearthed another disturbing

episode from Blymyre's past. Four years prior, he had persuaded a local farmer, Walter Keener, that he was cursed and coerced him into surrendering several acres of land to lift the hex. Fortunately, the intervention of the district attorney nullified the transaction, returning the land to the duped farmer.

Following their arrest, John Curry succumbed to the pressure of intense interrogation and confessed to the brutal murder of Nelson Rehmeyer. In his detailed admission, Curry implicated Blymyre and Wilbert Hess. According to the junior Hess, the trio had not only killed Rehmeyer but had callously doused his lifeless body in coal oil before igniting it to cover their crime.

John Curry

During Blymyre's trial, he maintained a bizarre defense, asserting that Rehmeyer was a formidable sorcerer and that, upon entering his home that fateful night to collect his hair, he witnessed goblins walking through the house.

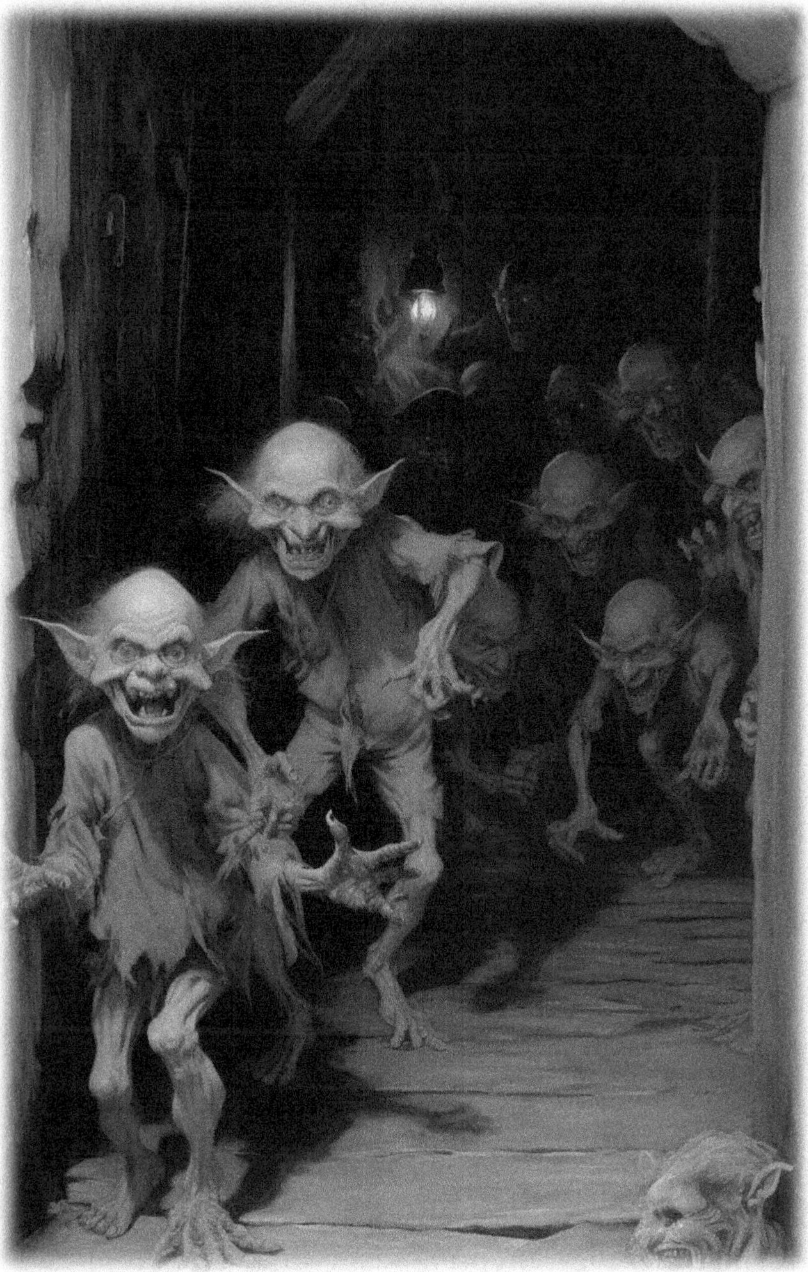

Blymyre, attempting to justify the murder, claimed that by eliminating Rehmeyer, he had done a favor to all farmers in the area. With Rehmeyer dead, there would longer be any farmers who had to live in fear of being hexed.

Passing the blame, he informed the jury that he had consulted Emma Knapp for guidance on helping the Hess family, who pointed to Nelson Rehmeyer who instructed him to get a lock of his hair. Allegedly, the initial intent was solely to acquire the hair, but the altercation escalated when the imposing six-foot-tall Rehmeyer resisted, forcing them to resort to lethal measures for self-defense.

A local doctor testified that Blymyre was mentally unstable on the night of the attack, contending that he was not in control of his actions and unable to distinguish right from wrong. Naturally, Blymyre's attorney played into this diagnosis.

During the trial, Blymyre's mother, Babula Blymyre, took the stand as a defense witness. She claimed that her son had fallen under the spell of a witch at a young age, revealing that even his sister had been similarly affected, leading to her untimely death. In her opinion, he was only doing what he thought was right by killing Rehmeyer.

On January 9, 1929, Blymyre was convicted of first-degree murder and sentenced to life in prison. Curry received a similar sentence for first-degree murder, while Wilbert Hess was sentenced to 10 years for second-degree murder. Despite their initial sentences, both Blymyre and Curry served only a portion of their prison terms.

Blymyre had his sentence commuted in 1953, while Hess served the entirety of his 10-year term. Curry, after a decade of imprisonment, was released, going on to serve in World War II and subsequently gaining recognition as a well-known artist.

The Witch of Ringtown Valley

In the heart of Pottsville, Pennsylvania, Susan Mummey, a middle-aged widow, held a dark reputation that transcended the boundaries of mere human existence. The tale begins with a bitter argument between Susan and her husband, Isaac in 1929.

In a fit of anger, Susan shouted as he left for work, "If you leave, you won't come back." Later that day a chilling prophecy unfolded as an explosion at the Dupont powder factory claimed her husband's life, along with several coworkers.

The story quickly spread around the area and the grieving widow became known as "The Witch of Ringtown Valley". It was believed she possessed powers capable of wreaking havoc on farm animals and inducing droughts to cripple those who wronged her. Susan's vengeful hexes were unleashed upon those who dared to cross her, leaving farms and families in ruin.

In the summer of 1927, 14-year-old Albert Shinsky found himself immersed in a chilling encounter while tending to his family's pigs on their farm. As he fed the pigs, he spotted Susan Mummey, one of his neighbors, strolling down a nearby path. Albert, familiar with Susan from previous encounters as he often cut through her farm on the way to his favorite summertime swimming hole, braced himself for an unexpected confrontation.

Approaching him with an air of authority, Susan immediately launched into a scolding, fueled by heightened agitation. The cause of her ire was the recent transgression of the Shinsky family's cows, which had breached a fence, finding their way onto Susan's farm. Amid the reprimands, Susan ominously declared, "I'll get you for this! You better watch out!" Her words hung in the air like an impending storm, foreboding trouble for the unsuspecting teenager.

As the verbal onslaught continued, Albert felt an abrupt, bone-chilling cold shoot through his body, followed by an unsettling fog that settled into the recesses of his mind. Unbeknownst to him, Susan, in a fit of anger, had cast a curse upon the young farmer. This malevolent hex plunged Albert into a nightmarish existence.

That very night, a spectral presence manifested itself in the form of a large black cat. Menacingly, it leaped onto Albert's bed, its sharp claws tearing into his flesh with a pain so unbearable that he attempted to scream, only to find his voice stifled. Astonishingly, come morning, his body bore no scars of the nocturnal assault.

Undeterred by the torment, Albert went to live with relatives in a nearby town, hoping to escape the clutches of the ominous feline apparition. To his dismay, the black cat persisted in haunting his nights, an unwelcome companion that defied the boundaries of place and kinship. Even a relocation to Newark provided no relief, as visions of Susan as well as her spectral companion continued to shadow Albert's every step. Terrifying dreams and a persistent fog in his mind pushed Albert into a deep depression. His ordeal worsened as he lost his ability to taste food, surviving solely on bread and milk. Desperate for relief from the malevolent visions that plagued him, Albert Shinsky embarked on a journey to Hazelton to seek the counsel of an Indian man rumored to possess mystical powers. Upon arriving, Albert poured out his troubled soul, detailing the torment inflicted by Susan Mummey's curse.

The Indian, shrouded in an air of spiritual wisdom, instructed Albert to fetch his pillow. Trusting in the hope of liberation, Albert hurried home, retrieved the pillow, and presented it to the mystic. To his bewilderment, the Indian proceeded to tear the pillow up before his eyes, proclaiming that this act should bring an end to the haunting visions. Unfortunately, Susan and the black cat continued to haunt him each night.

Undeterred, Albert returned to the mystic, ready to undertake any ritual that might sever the bonds of the hex. Instructed to walk barefoot and cast any stones found over his left shoulder, Albert diligently adhered to the prescribed regimen. Despite his earnest efforts, the spectral apparitions persisted, refusing to relinquish their grip on his tortured psyche. When Albert went back again, the Indian, with an air of solemnity, advised Albert that when the ominous cat and Susan materialized in the darkened hours, he should cry out to God for deliverance. Strangely, this plea offered temporary respite, but the terror soon rendered Albert mute in the face of the nocturnal apparitions.

In a final, desperate revelation, the Indian conveyed a chilling ultimatum to Albert — to find relief from the curse, he would have to take the life of Susan Mummey.

Fearing the moral weight of killing someone, Albert sought an alternative path to freedom from Susan's hex. Guided by the counsel of a local minister, he found himself at Locust Mountain Hospital, where medical scrutiny deemed him healthy, providing no tangible relief to his afflicted mind. Following the advice of a minister from New Jersey, Albert embarked on pilgrimages to Catholic shrines in the area, hoping for divine intervention. Despite these spiritual endeavors, the haunting specters of the cat and Susan persisted, casting shadows over his restless nights.

In pursuit of a semblance of normalcy, Albert resettled in Shenandoah, scratching out a modest existence by shuttling miners to and from the mines. Yet, the curse lingered, casting a perpetual pall over his daily existence.

In January 1934, a revelation unfolded for the beleaguered 24-year-old Albert Shinsky when an otherworldly visitation transpired. An angelic apparition materialized before him, delivering a sinister message — Susan was consorting with the devil, and the only way to stop her was death. Fueled by the desperate hope of breaking the curse that bound him, Albert meticulously devised a plan.

Seeking a weapon, he borrowed a .12-gauge shotgun from a friend. Under the cloak of night on March 17,

1934, Albert steered his vehicle to a desolate field, positioned a half-mile from Susan's dwelling. Cloaked in darkness, he traveled the uneven terrain, the weight of the shotgun in his hands underscoring the gravity of his intent.

Approaching Susan's residence, Albert, armed with the firearm, navigated through the fields. Peering through a window on the front porch, he observed a domestic scene — Susan's adopted 24-year-old daughter, Tavilla, tending to a boarder nursing an injured foot. Susan, a fleeting figure, entered and exited the room. Seizing the opportune moment, Albert raised his shotgun to the window, the cold metal reflecting the moonlight, and discharged a fatal blast. Susan crumpled to the ground; life extinguished by the violent echo in the stillness of the night.

With a chilling determination, Albert swiftly moved to another window, firing another shot into the darkness. His commanding voice pierced the ensuing silence as he ordered everyone in the house to remain inside, threatening further violence if his commands were ignored. Abruptly, he retreated back to his car, driving a short distance away where he perceived safety.

Overwhelmed by a potent cocktail of emotions, Albert stepped out of the vehicle into the solitude of the night. Tears of relief and euphoria streamed down his face as he embraced the newfound sense of liberation. The moonlit expanse became a stage for his cathartic dance, a symbolic shedding of the shackles that had bound him for so long.

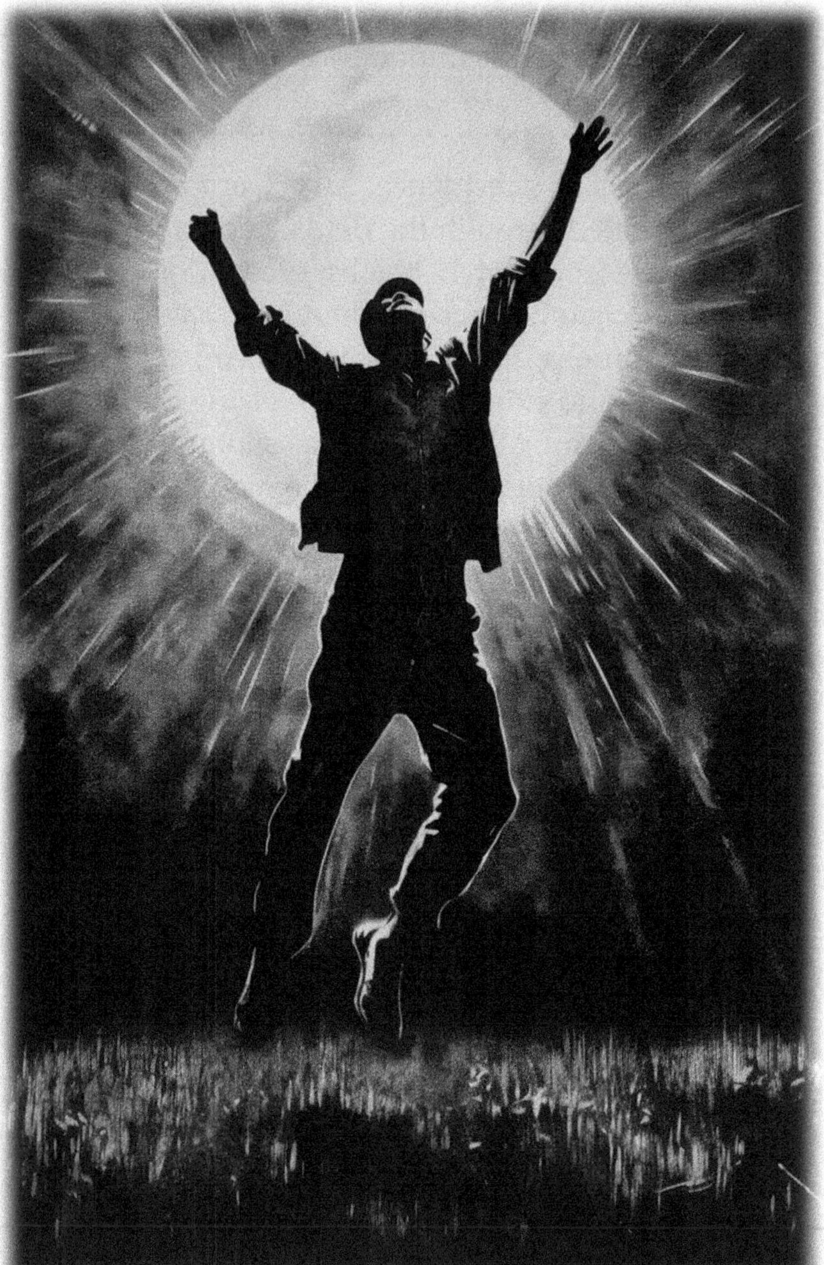

Slowly, the oppressive weight lifted, and Albert, bathed in moonlight, felt the gradual return of normalcy. Driven by this newfound freedom, he embarked on a journey to his girlfriend's house, eager to share the news of his freedom from Susan's curse.

As dawn painted the sky, the aftermath of Albert's nocturnal odyssey unfolded. Tavilla, Susan's adopted daughter, shaken by the terror of the night, mustered the courage to contact the police. The ensuing investigation revealed a gruesome truth — a large "pumpkin ball" slug, typically used to hunt bears, had embedded itself in Susan's stomach.

Tragically for Albert, a young boy residing near Susan's farm chanced upon his strange celebration, keenly remembering the license plate number of the vehicle he had been driving. When the police commenced their investigation, the astute boy recounted the peculiar scene he had witnessed. A few days elapsed before the wheels of justice caught up with Albert, who vehemently disavowed any knowledge of the heinous act when confronted by law enforcement.

However, the facade of innocence crumbled the following day, as Albert, in a state of emotional turmoil, divulged a confession that echoed with supernatural overtones. "I heard a voice from the sky say, 'shoot that woman' and I did," Shinsky confessed. He painted a harrowing picture of a hexed existence, haunted by black cats with eyes aflame, descending from the celestial realm to assail him. These feline apparitions invaded his room, clawing at his body, with one even threatening to suffocate him with its fur. The only perceived recourse, according to Albert, was the violent death of Susan to shatter the malevolent curse.

Following the murder, Albert astonishingly asserted a restoration of his sensory and mental faculties. He claimed a resumption of taste, a newfound clarity of thought, and an emergence of a sense of manhood. In a testament to an unexpected turn of events, Albert harbored plans for matrimony with his sweetheart, Selena Bernstel, on Easter Sunday in April.

Astonishingly, despite the looming murder charge, Selena staunchly stood by Albert, contending that he had undergone a transformative metamorphosis. She asserted that the man who had refrained from kissing her during their courtship now embraced a newfound joy, making love for the first time on the night following Susan's death.

Within the confines of his jail cell, Albert's saga took an even more surreal turn as individuals from the community surfaced with claims of their own afflictions under Susan's alleged hex. The tendrils of her supernatural influence seemed to have touched the lives of others, further complicating the already convoluted narrative surrounding the enigmatic Susan Mummey.

Paul Stauffer, a local miner, found himself ensnared in Susan's alleged hex after taking his mules to fetch water from a creek on her farm. As Paul crossed her path, Susan's gaze seemed to linger for what felt like an eternity, and an unsettling feeling immediately gripped him. Despite this, Paul continued taking his mules to the creek, only to witness their agitated behavior in Susan's presence. The distressed animals would buck and act erratically, necessitating a peculiar ritual for their appeasement – a prayer followed by the cursing of the witch's name.

One day, following a severe storm, Susan summoned Paul to assist her in extracting water from her cellar. With reluctance, Paul descended into the dim confines, where he stumbled upon three jars containing the macabre remnants of deceased piglets. Susan, discovering his inspection, approached with anger, thrusting Paul into a trance-like state, feeling as though a myriad of daggers pierced his body. He hastily retreated, haunted thereafter by nocturnal visions of Susan standing in his room, a spectral specter staring ominously.

Upon Susan's death, Paul experienced a transformative release from the oppressive fog that had shrouded his existence. Fatigue relinquished its grip, and he candidly expressed to a reporter, "I feel fine and full of pep as though my brains are coming to life again."

George Drumheller also fell victim to Susan's curse, enduring an entire summer of clouded thoughts that banished him from the confines of his own home. Driven to desperation by the pain and discomfort, George attempted to drown himself in the creek and contemplated hanging. His wife intervened just in time, saving him from the brink. George, in turn, diagnosed Albert, sharing the revelation of the hex that plagued them.

Seeking solace, George consulted a native American man named Beau Eagle, colloquially known as "a pow-wow man." Beau Eagle conducted a ceremony that provided momentary relief but cautioned George that true liberation from the curse hinged on Susan's death.

Susan's purported hex also extended to George's stepson, Bill Shoup, during his childhood. Caught playing on her property, Bill faced Susan's wrath – she threw rocks at him and issued death threats, marking the young boy with the malevolent touch of her alleged supernatural powers.

Despite the extraordinary delusions that the authorities believed afflicted Albert Shinsky, District Attorney Leroy Enterline asserted his intent to pursue a first-degree murder verdict in court. Enterline insisted that Albert would be tried as a sane individual, further declaring he would pursue the electric chair.

Dr. A. I. Baron delved into Albert's psyche during a two-hour jail visit as he awaited trial. Baron's diagnosis depicted Albert as suffering from a split personality and emotional instability. Advocating for psychiatric treatment over incarceration, Baron characterized Albert as "five different people," each personality locked in internal conflict. Stunted in emotional growth beyond puberty, Albert's imaginative extrovert tendencies were explored, with underlying issues regarding his parents, particularly a perceived favoritism from his mother towards his father.

In contrast, Dr. Walter G. Bowers from the Schuylkill County Hospital for Mental Disease contended that the young man's delusions unequivocally signaled insanity. Calling for a sanity commission, Bowers aimed to formally assess Shinsky's mental state. If deemed insane, Shinsky would be committed to Farview Hospital in Waymart, with a potential return for trial upon the restoration of sanity. Bowers also highlighted the hereditary nature of mental illness in Albert's family, citing his brother's earlier commitment to an asylum.

Facing inquiries about the possibility of insanity, Shinsky scoffed, considering the idea ridiculous. Asserting his normalcy and liberation from Mrs. Mummey's hex, Shinsky found an ally in his sweetheart, Selina Bernstel, who vouched for his soundness.

Despite initial reluctance, prison warden William Watson, succumbing to public pressure, joined forces with District Attorney Enterline to petition Judge Henry Houck for a lunacy commission. On April 12, the commission's report declared Albert Shinsky insane, leading to an order from Judge Houck for his transfer to the state asylum at Farview. In jail, Albert claimed Susan began haunting him again, resorting to standing on his head and sleeping on a board to drive away the alleged "hex devils." Upon transfer to Fairview, Albert claimed Susan ceased appearing.

In July 1947, after over a decade at Farview, Albert Shinsky believed himself fully cured and sought release. Despite a petition, his release was denied in October after asylum doctors opposed it. A subsequent 1962 petition faced opposition from a doctor, and an independent psychiatric evaluation confirmed Shinsky's continued insanity, prompting him to remain in the asylum.

In 1976, Albert Shinsky, now 62, was deemed fit for trial by a judge. Transferred to Wernersville State Hospital, the trial concluded with a quiet resolution in March. With principal witnesses deceased, a nol prosse motion by District Attorney Richard Russell meant Shinsky would not be prosecuted. After 42 years of confinement, the man who allegedly killed the Witch of Ringtown Valley was a free man.

Shinsky's freedom, however, proved fleeting. Declining physical health led to his admission to a nursing home in Shenandoah in February 1983, and he passed away three months later.

And as for Albert Shinsky's beloved fiancé who stood behind him despite the mounting legal challenges; Selina Bernstel, eventually married another man and relocated to Bucks County.

The New York Necromancers

Scientific Psychology

In the early 1930s, a peculiar rumor took hold in the bustling streets of New York City, weaving a tale around Ida Rubin, a mysterious woman residing on 65th Street. Whispers circulated that Ida was not just an ordinary woman but a witch and a necromancer, capable of wielding supernatural powers to influence love lives and bestow good fortune. Ida, a mother of three, operated from her home on 65th Street, where she sold trinkets and purported good luck charms containing hair, bones, and dried blood from a dead murderer – elements she claimed to acquire by raiding local cemeteries.

Marie Ambrose, a 30-year-old woman yearning to secure a marriage proposal from her long-time boyfriend, found herself at a crossroads. Despite her earnest efforts, her boyfriend seemed reluctant to take the decisive step towards marriage.

Frustrated and on the brink of despair, Marie vented her concerns one day at the beauty parlor.

In the midst of her lamentations, a lady at the beauty parlor wrote down the address for Ida Rubin, singing praises of the witch and the remarkable assistance she had provided. Marie, initially dismissive of witchcraft and magic, expressed skepticism. Undeterred, the lady encouraged Marie to observe her surroundings, pointing out seemingly overweight and disagreeable women who had successfully attracted wealthy and attractive husbands through magical means. This narrative planted a seed in Marie's mind, suggesting that resorting to magic might be the key to winning a man's heart.

Marie thought about it for a while and as her boyfriend dragged his feet and seemed to be disinterested, one night she found Ida's address and paid her a visit.

When Marie consulted with Ida, the witch explained her three distinct methods: "scientific psychology," an economical option; spiritualism, a more costly alternative; and magic, the priciest due to the expenses associated with the required materials. Ida assured Marie that inducing affection in her boyfriend would be a straightforward task. The proposed solution involved bringing the young man to Ida's home, where she would cast a spell on him. However, Marie harbored reservations about revealing her consultation with a witch to her boyfriend, fearing it might jeopardize their relationship.

Expressing her frustration, Ida insisted that if Marie intended to cast spells on a young man without his consent, a fee of $100 was imperative to ensure secrecy. Alarmed, Marie recognized the necessity of paying to safeguard the clandestine nature of her visits to the witch. Thus, she commenced payments for Ida's services.

Marie's visits to Ida involved payments for purported charms that were believed to enhance her romantic fortunes. Among these was a charm bag, designed to be worn around her neck, containing Hebrew writings on a piece of paper. Additionally, Ida supplied Marie with a powder purportedly made from the bones of a murderer, instructing her to sprinkle it on her boyfriend's shoulders when he wasn't looking. Despite following these instructions, Marie encountered no success. As her financial resources dwindled, Ida resorted to threats of disclosing the magical interventions to Marie's boyfriend. Fearing the consequences, Marie pleaded with Ida, who, in turn, provided her with a business card from someone in New York who could lend her money.

Marie continued her visits to Ida, making payments ranging from $5 to $10 per week beginning in 1932, hoping to transform her love life. On one occasion, after bringing money, Marie was invited into Ida's home for a ceremony involving lit candles and mystical phrases. This ritual was purported to reinvigorate their relationship and deepen Marie's boyfriend's undying love for her.

Realizing the inefficacy of Ida's spells, Marie ceased her visits and payments. In January 1935, Ida attributed the lack of affection from Marie's boyfriend to a rival witch, claiming his family had paid the rival more to curse their relationship. Ida insisted on a higher payment of $500 for better results, citing the rarity and premium cost of acquiring genuine undiluted blood and bone fragments from a murderer.

In compliance, Marie delivered the payment to Ida a few days later, prompting Ida to instruct her to bring the previously given charms to Floyd Bennett Airfield. In a clandestine meeting under the cover of darkness, Ida guided a desperate Marie in throwing the white powder into the wind, a strange and unique ritual purported to summon the ghost of an evil man. The spirit, once summoned, would torment Marie's boyfriend, rendering him broken and incomplete without her, eventually compelling him to propose marriage. Despite her eagerness to get married, Marie hesitated at the prospect of invoking an evil spirit but eventually complied by tossing the powder into the wind.

Even though she had followed all of Ida's directions, the young man kept distancing himself Marie until finally breaking off the relationship.

Once again, a heartbroken and devastated Marie, returned to Ida for help. Ida, seizing the opportunity, demanded $1,000. When Marie balked, Ida threatened to cast a death curse on Marie and her elderly mother. Fearing for her mother's safety, Marie handed over $500 on October 16, 1936. However, faced with a pressing bill, Marie requested a partial refund, leading Ida to agree to return $175 under the condition that Marie would repay it later.

Ida Rubin

Upon learning of Marie's problems with Ida, her family, aware of the potential scam, threatened to involve the police unless she retrieved her money. Feeling the pressure, Marie approached Ida, who didn't want to involve law enforcement, nervously offered her $700. At this moment, Marie realized she was being scammed and promptly reported Ida's fraudulent activities to the police, joined by two friends who had also fallen victim to the schemes.

Christina Tortora, one of Marie's friends, disclosed her own encounter with Ida. She had paid $650 for her mother's well-being and an additional $700 to have a spell cast on her ex-husband, who had left town with all the money from their joint bank account in 1933. Despite the payments, neither the husband returned, nor could Ida locate him. Ida justified the funds as payment for "lessons in psychology and divine metaphysics," resulting in her being charged with grand larceny.

Rose Davis, another friend of Marie, paid Ida $525 to turn her luck around after a divorce. However, like the others, Rose's life didn't get any easier despite the payments to the New York necromancer.

During the trial, Ida vehemently denied practicing black magic and instead portrayed herself as a "divine metaphysic." While asserting that she graduated from "The College of Divine Metaphysics" in the Midwest, she confessed on the stand that she did not attend the school and was tutored by a graduate after paying them $640. Ida allegedly received a diploma by mail.

In a plea deal, Ida admitted guilt to extorting only $500, disavowing any threats against Marie or her mother. Acknowledging some of the payments from Marie, she justified it as a fee for "psychology instruction."

Ultimately, Ida was placed on probation and gradually faded into the obscurity of everyday life leaving behind a trail of deception, manipulation, and shattered hopes.

Desperation

It sounded absurd when Ida Rubin told Marie Ambrose that a rival witch had cast a more powerful spell on her relationship with her boyfriend. However, during that time, another alleged witch was in the Bronx helping locals with their problems.

Marie Crescenzo, a mother of five born in Italy, migrated to New York in the 1920s. Initially known for her herbal concoctions that aided the sick, Crescenzo's reputation blossomed, attracting those seeking assistance in matters of the heart and beyond.

Marie Crescenzo

Josephine Alfano was a young woman whose love story became a tragic saga. At the tender age of 15, Josephine fell deeply in love with Benny Gable in Italy and made plans to marry him. However, Benny had to go to New York to find a job and he quickly began climbing the ladder and drifted from his teenage lover in Italy. When Josephine moved to New York six years later, she discovered that Benny had fallen for another woman.

Desperation drove Josephine to seek the help of Marie Crescenzo in November 1929. Crescenzo, claiming to possess the ability to reignite Benny's love, informed Josephine that the spirits demanded payment for their services. With scraped-together funds totaling $400, Josephine paid Crescenzo for charms and rituals. Despite subsequent payments amounting to $300, Benny remained unresponsive.

As Josephine's desperation grew, so did Crescenzo's demands. An additional $150 for a supposedly more powerful charm yielded no results. Even worse, Benny abruptly moved back to Italy, leaving Josephine even more heartbroken. Fueled by anguish and a sense of betrayal, she sought help once again from Marie Crescenzo.

In an emotional whirlwind, Josephine stormed into Crescenzo's home, unleashing a torrent of accusations and threats to involve the authorities. It was in this charged moment that Crescenzo disclosed a revelation that would plunge Josephine deeper into the labyrinth of mysticism and despair. Another sorceress, armed with access to even more potent spirits, was engaging in a cosmic battle for Benny's affections on behalf of another woman.

Yet, in a macabre twist, Crescenzo offered a glimmer of hope amidst the shadows. She promised access to the "most powerful spirits in the universe" that would wage a metaphysical war for Benny's love. However, to counter the rival witch, Crescenzo asserted the need for an extra $200 to obtain the essential supplies for casting formidable love spells.

In a desperate plea, Josephine, grasping at any chance of reclaiming Benny's heart, parted with yet another two hundred dollars.

After a week or two, Josephine found herself back at Crescenzo's doorstep. Crescenzo handed her a package purportedly containing the ashes of a recently departed young woman. Instructed to go to the Hudson River, Josephine was tasked with releasing the ashes into the water while chanting an incantation, "Benny, my love, come back to me."

The ritual, laced with desperation and fueled by a flicker of hope, unfolded on the banks of the Hudson River. Josephine, a puppet in the hands of Crescenzo's arcane promises, cast the ashes into the water, the rhythmic flow of the river carrying away the remnants of a life once lived.

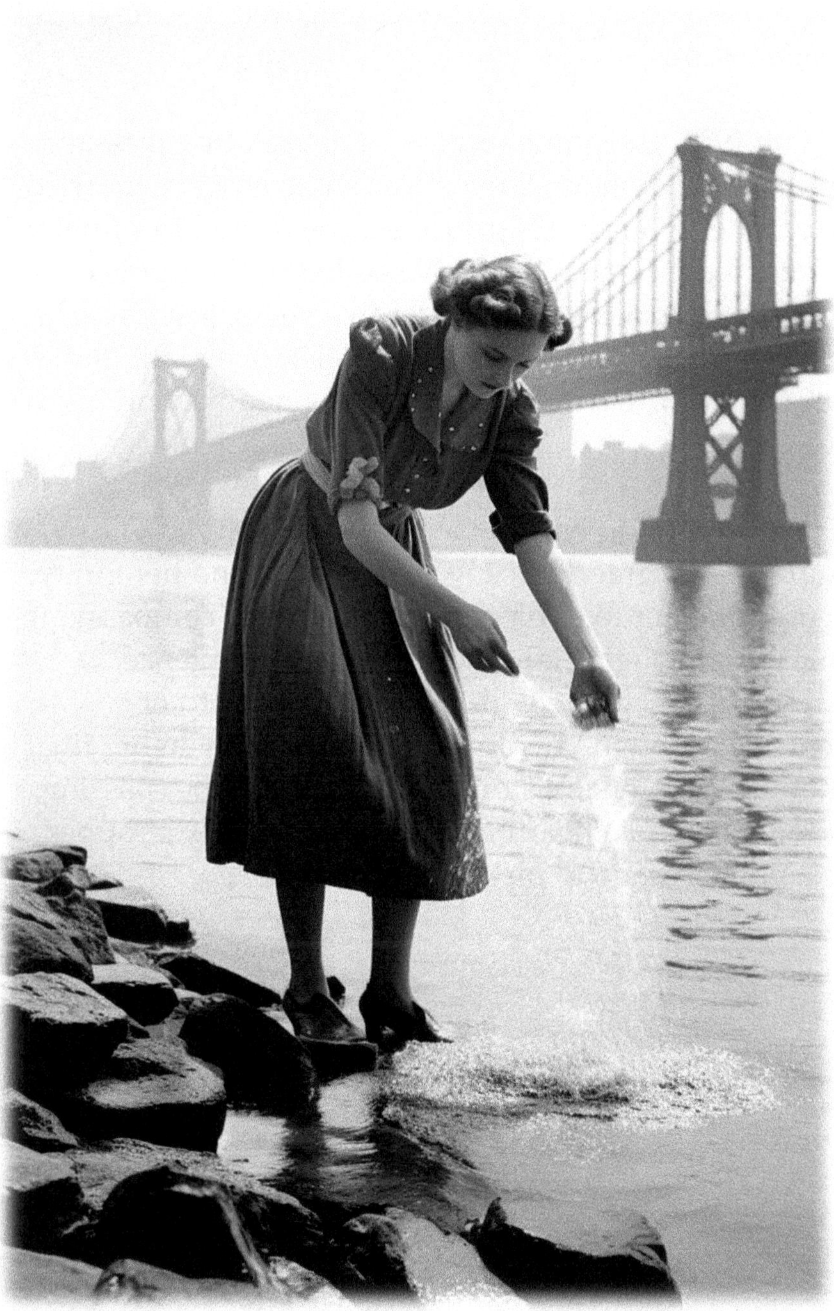

Unfortunately for Josephine, the desired outcome remained elusive, and Benny's heart remained impervious to the mystical tides conjured by Crescenzo's machinations.

In late 1935, Josephine received a devastating message from Benny, announcing he was engaged to be married to another woman. Heartbroken, she turned to a family friend, a policeman, who advised her to file a police report against Crescenzo. Over five years, Josephine had paid Crescenzo $2,700, a substantial sum equating to $60,000 in 2024, and still Benny remained beyond her reach.

Crescenzo found herself facing a trial, charged with third-degree grand larceny. The court found her guilty, sentencing her to two years in prison. Yet, compassion intervened when, eight months into her sentence, Crescenzo fell gravely ill. A judge commuted her sentence, allowing her to be with her family in her final months. Crescenzo's story concluded with her passing, leaving behind a heartbroken and financially strapped Josephine Alfano to pick up the pieces.